A
MARRIED MAN'S
SURVIVAL GUIDE

Cover Photo:

Cover photo by Keith Ducatel, Copyright © 2010, All rights reserved.
www.KeithDucatel.com

Keith Ducatel
Unit 3B
50 Westminster Bridge Rd,
London
SE1 7QY

Pictured in the photo are English explorer Ed Stafford and his guide
Cho Sanchez. At the time of the photograph, Ed was attempting
to become the first human to have walked from the source of the
Amazon River to its mouth. In such a foreign and, at times, hostile
environment, Ed relied on those native to the area to provide him
guidance. We felt it to be an apt metaphor for those venturing into
the challenging world of marriage.

ISBN: 1453706291
EAN13: 9781453706299
LCCN: 2010910578

A
Married Man's
Survival Guide

David Plante
&
Kris Girrell

"Your task is not to seek for love, but merely to seek and find all the barriers within yourself that you have built against it."

Rumi

TABLE OF CONTENTS

SECTION 1

WATER AND FOOD (FOR THOUGHT)

"Why does a man take it for granted that a girl who flirts with him
wants him to kiss her—when nine times out of ten,
*she **only** wants him to kiss her?"*
Helen Rowland

If you have ever been caught in a riptide, tossed from a raft in white water, or lost in the middle of a huge blowdown in the forest, you know that fighting it is the worst thing you can do. You and nature are one; she provides food and water as well as the river, the tide, and the jungle. The very thing that threatens your life can sustain it. Your marriage is not much different from the jungle, and your wife not too far afield from Mother Nature herself.

(Kris and Dave)

INTRODUCTION — WHY WE WROTE THIS

You're lost. You know you're lost because you're at the bottom of the same rock slope that you scrambled up yesterday and the day before. You didn't even notice that you were going downhill before you got back here. How did this happen?

You thought you were prepared for this journey. You've done lots of shorter hikes, you survived those, and you thought you had learned from them. And you thought this one was going to be the same, only longer. But now you know that you were wrong; you just don't have the skills you need to survive, let alone thrive in this wilderness.

Sound familiar? Maybe you've never been lost in the woods before, but there's another situation that can make you feel like that—marriage. It's totally foreign territory for most men, and many men haven't had training from the proper role models. Even if you had a great father or other role model, the landscape of marriage and male-female relations in general have changed dramatically in the past generation, and many of the lessons you learned may be out of date now. Maybe you've had short-term relationships with a few girlfriends, or this is your second or third marriage, but what you've learned from them probably doesn't help you now; in fact, prior experience from unsuccessful relationships just gets in the way.

We're guessing that if you're reading this, you're feeling at least a little like the lost hiker, and that's a good thing—you won't find your way unless you admit that you're lost and then get some help. That's what we're here for: first, to show you how really lost you are, because most married men don't have a clue—including us, the authors, before we started to really focus on our marriages and get help from wise mentors; and second, to help give you the skills you need to succeed at this grueling trek called a long-term committed relationship with a woman.

Our cover photo is real, just like your marriage. One of the men, Ed Stafford, is a modern-day explorer trying to become the first human to walk the entire length of the Amazon River. Ed is shown conferring with his guide, Cho Sanchez, after a particularly challenging day. Like anyone venturing into an unknown territory, Stafford relies on the wisdom of those who have been in the territory before. At the time of the photograph, Stafford had been walking for nearly two years and anticipated at least nine more months of hacking, wading, and walking. But he was committed and in it for the long haul. All the rest—dealing with the bugs, the risks, food supplies, and the unknown—are just what you handle when you are committed.

We organized this guide in sections like a survival guide. First there are the basics of food and water, which for us are the stuff of married life—our women. But having decided to venture into a long-term committed relationship, our next vital need is a sense of direction. This compass is our men, and in particular, our mentors and guides.

Just like any long trek, we have to be concerned with safety and shelter and, in the case of marriage, with providing that for our companion. If we fail to provide a safe place for our woman's emotional being, the relationship cannot survive long. More importantly, if we fail there is no shot of having the deep intimacy and sexuality of a loving relationship. Thus, our next section is dedicated to keeping her warm and sexually fired up.

But no survival guide would be complete without some dedicated time spent on emergencies. We break these into two groups: the first aid required for minor scrapes, and then serious help for the life-threatening situations of separation and divorce. The guide concludes with two important sections. Keeping fit details some of the disciplines and practices that will keep you in shape for this long journey of committed marriage, and a set of fun, interesting, and at times whimsical things to do that will keep a smile on your wife's face and you in a great place!

Another thing we would like to note here is why we think it is important to write this guide. There are four important reasons:

Most marriages are doomed. Statistics show that the life expectancy of a modern-day marriage is not at all promising[1]* and that is mainly because we have created a society of self-serving comfort and convenience. And marriage is NOT convenient. Marriage is fraught with problems inherent in the simple fact that two people are involved (not to mention the fact that those two people happen to have some very distinct differences that go well beyond their

---

1 According to Forest Institute of Professional Psychology the divorce rate in America: for first marriage is 41%; for second marriage is 60%; and for third marriage is 73% (from http://www.divorcerate.org/, accessed August 2010)

basic plumbing). This guide discusses how to deal with those differences and how to work your part of the marriage deal. You might not like what we have to offer or what we insist is your job, but get over it—or don't buy the damn book in the first place. We seriously doubt that we will get rich from selling books—we care too much about helping men to let that get in the way!

Men are not taught about their roles. Our nuclear family system and socialization structures have been blown up and are now nonexistent. In times past, elders socialized and trained men and boys. But in today's society, the family unit is scattered and most neighborhoods are in lockdown. Men are no longer trained in the art of being a man let alone on how to be a husband and father. The old service groups like Elks, Moose, Eagles, Shriners, Masons, and so on are on the decline and most men live, as Henry David Thoreau called them, "lives of quiet desperation." They are alone and separated from their men, feminized and legislated into numbness. This guide is a collection of men's wisdom—from men with successful marriages, for men who want to be successful.

Men are relationship deficient (for the most part). Especially when it comes to doing what it takes to keep a creature as complex as a woman charmed, happy, and thriving in your presence. Two parts of this come into play: one is that we men actually think we relate to others well when we do things like playing sports, going camping and fishing, or watching a show together. That is not relating—that is doing shit together. Women crave relationships and have wound up in contractual bonds with men (probably only because their biology seduced them into thinking men might be able to do this relationship thing). We suck at relationship skills. Hell, one of us is a psychologist and freely admits that he sucks at it. But secondly, we once challenged our team to come up with a list of ways to court our women and keep them smiling and most of the others could list only a few (five if they were good). This guide has 250 such ideas designed to fuel your relationship. So we offer this up as a starter kit of relationship maintenance tools.

We are committed to marital success. We regularly coach men on their marriages. It is something we are committed to. Both of us have answered calls at 2:00 a.m. or 4:00 a.m. to stand between couples' often violent domestic quarrels. Both of us routinely coach and mentor young men seeking to get married or, after the fact—having just gotten married. Both of us have helped men turn around separations and divorces to see families reunite. We are committed to marital successes and especially to helping men win, BIG, in their lives.

Our aim is to have fun, teach some tools, and share the collected wisdom of some selected, wizened elders, from our own combined half century of marriage experiences, as well as our lessons from failures, and big successes. But enough about us; what about you?

Why are you reading this book? You may find yourself in relationship with a woman and wondering how you got here and how you are going to stay here. You don't really know the lay of the land and cannot seem to figure out the rules. Maybe you are a bunch of years down the marriage road and suddenly find it dry and dusty and lifeless. Sex is boring or nonexistent and the regular routines are—well, just that—routine.

Relax—you are not alone. But you need some help in dealing with this relationship because you were not trained in relationship management. This guide is designed to help you survive this wonderful yet at times painful life you are living. It is aimed at more than merely surviving—our aim is to help you keep it vital (or to revitalize it), alive and juicy.

Voices of the Masters — Throughout this Guide we will insert occasional quotes from some of the men—whom refer to as **Master Guides**—in this territory. These are men with 25+ years of successful, monogamous marriage that we interviewed in researching material for this guide book. The *Voice of the Master* will appear as a small shaded text box like this one.

CAUTION

First and foremost, we want to go on record as saying that
neither of us is practicing as a licensed psychologist, nor are
we pretending to be research authorities. If that is what you
need in order to be able to accept these principles as truths then you
might as well put this book back on the shelf you got it from. We
are just two men; married men, committed to other men, and passing on that which has been made available to us from our mentors
and from our own, hard-won learning.

The recommendations and ideas in this guide, while useful to
us and the men we have worked with, may not be universally ap-
plicable. We clearly recognize that every man is somewhat different
and every woman is perhaps more so. Thus, not everything that
we claim will apply uniformly to all marriages. Take us with a
grain of salt! Your marriage is yours and is unique to you and your
wife—your problems and concerns, your joys and disappointments
are unique to the two of you. We make some rather strong assertions, and push toward a specific regimen for success. It is hard
work at times but we think you will find most of these principles

and tactics useful and effective. It is in that spirit—as brothers and fellow travelers down this path that we offer up these ideas.

However, you still might not want to read this book. Really. We are certain to say something that may piss you off, make you feel good and bad at the same time, make you end up wondering why you ever entered into a relationship with a woman in the first place, and then, just when you least want it, we will cram the ugly truth into your face. Certainly not what one might call casual reading, don't you think? This guide is an opportunity to take on some new disciplines as a man, and work at them—and it will be hard work. None of us likes hard work, we just are not built that way, and we would wager that you are the same. Hard work requires sacrifice, and when you make sacrifices, you run the risk of succeeding or failing. Winning is great and losing sucks, but we tend to learn only from risking (and often failing). If you take what you read here and integrate it as part of your life, you may be challenged, but we are certain that both you and your female counterpart will benefit. And the benefit will be huge.

Nonetheless, this is not meant to be a how-to book. If you think you can open it and rip out a page and try to do something that will make the relationship better, and then put it down until the next time you think you need it, you are sadly mistaken. This guide is meant to help you develop a way of being around surviving in a relationship, and in that way of being, you can have a productive, healthy relationship that you know you have given your best to.

So make your decision: Are you up for the job? Then let's get to it!

AN INTRODUCTION FOR WOMEN WHO CARE TO READ THIS BOOK

*"A wise woman puts a grain of sugar into
everything she says to a man, and takes a grain of
salt with everything he says to her."*

Helen Rowland

Welcome to our world. We encourage you to read this book, but we do not expect that you will agree with all of our assertions. You may at times be confused because it's men talking to men in men's language. This section, however, might help you understand how we generally view our brothers and answer some of your questions about how men see the world.

We assume that you have more than a passing interest in men and in the message of this book; that is, that men can both commit to and be successful in marriage. Many women have asked us questions over the umpteen years we have been engaged in men's work and marriage coaching. Regardless of the focus of those questions—marriage, recreation, or companionship—at the heart of every question was, "What makes men tick?"

Just in case you had not noticed, men come in all shapes and sizes and likewise (more apropos to this discussion) men come in all levels of development and levels of maturity or sophistication. Now to further confuse you, we have to say that, as men, we do not distinguish among them. One of the things we have learned in our years of men's work is that we really ARE all the same. So when we are asked, "Do you know any wonderful men like you (aw shucks), who—you know—aren't married and aren't, um, well, jerks?" Our typical answer is a) nope, we are all jerks of some kind, b) I know some single men, but what are you looking for, or c) I'm confused.

The problem stems from the simple fact that we see all men as just men and from what we call the "he's ours" syndrome. You see, every group of men has one man who is (for example) cheap—like, when we get together to watch the game, he never brings the chips he said he would. Every group has one nerd or one of more nefarious history, and our response—when asked why the cheapskate, nerd, or sleaze is tolerated—invariably is, "Every group has one; he's ours." So when you ask your male friends for distinctions between levels or types of men, they will either refuse, diffuse, or get confused. Let's not go there. So if you are asking (or thinking) what population of men might this book be written for, we will simply, matter-of-factly answer you—it is for our men, for all men. We do not distinguish.

But you may still want to know what types of men get married, and what they bring as their unique "gift" to the marriage, and, of course, we do want to help you out. So we put forth the following classification system for identifying men, how to recognize them in their natural habitat, their evolution/development issues, maturity, spirituality, and of course viability as a mate—all in one easy-to-understand system. Much of our thinking on this was spurred by Rob Becker's one-man Broadway and touring show *Defending the Caveman*, well worth seeing a dozen times—especially with a bunch of couples. Becker traces the differences, quite comically, back to our prehistoric beginnings. He contends that it all started with the cavemen. We agree that we are all cavemen, but perhaps of differing types. Let us explain:[2]*

Australopithecus (A). As the first to come outside of his cave, A is, probably to your thinking, the least evolved man. A is in charge of his territory; he knows how to build and fix anything. He is the consummate **home builder** and do-it-yourselfer. But our knuckle-dragging brother isn't one who is much into conversation, more likely he'd rather sit silently for eight hours fishing, than ask you how you are. Spirituality is simple for A: he worships football heroes and if he is a churchgoer, he hears or digests little beyond God is good and it is bad to kill. As for sex, it's on his terms and pretty much an athletic event. A loves the smell of it, the sweat of it, and the noise of it. A just wants to be rewarded for his job of protecting the cave. Forget much about love and money, just make a home with him and settle down; A can be counted on to never stray and to be a hard worker and a fierce defender of you and your offspring. At his best, he is salt of the earth, steadfast, and strong. At his worst, A is, well, lewd, crude, and a knuckle-dragger who scratches his nuts a lot.

Neanderthal (N). N is a bit trickier to figure out. He has a skeptical awareness that borders on cynical. Having left the cave behind he is distrustful and on guard. He will find the negative in

---

2 Note to our more scientifically conscientious readers: This section is not meant to be accurate or in any way reflective of chronology and anthropological evidence of cave dwelling. We are speaking figuratively in a way that makes sense to you and to our average brother.

anything, anyone, or any situation. Nothing is good enough, strong enough, or lasting enough for him. As such he is the "canary in the mine" and the first to sniff out trouble or bullshit. He is the consummate truth-teller, regardless of what you think of him. He calls it as he sees it, but, on the good side, he'll keep us all out of trouble because his ultimate concern is **safety**. N has high ethical standards that not even he can uphold, though he tries to with every breath. Perhaps that's why he comes across as negative. Sex and spirituality "enjoy" the same fate. Sex is inadequate at best and God might be in question as well. However, N is shrewd in business and can be a classic "bring home the bacon" type of man. At his best, N will throw himself in harm's way to save you from the oncoming bus. He is good in his core and as value driven as the day is long. It's just that his delivery sucks. At his worst, N is an arrogant prick that can drain the joy out of your life if you aren't aware of his context and rock-solid values.

Homo Erectus (H). Oh you think this means "upright man" but, in actuality, H is upright in another sense. H is the sex machine among us—always up and hard and ready to go. H is the alpha male. H is the conqueror. H will sweep you off your feet and make you blush at your thoughts. If you can keep him under your sexual charms for 1001 nights, you may have a shot at keeping this man, but be aware that others of your gender have their eyes on him too. H has no real allegiance to others. H is after **success**: defined as wealth, power, and trophies. You may like the financial prowess or leadership capacity of this powerful man but judge him more through his actions and not his words. If your intention is marriage, H needs to be focused on his purpose. You must be willing to take second seat to his purpose and support him in his quest. At his best, H is a leader (the trick, as we said, being keeping him focused on a purpose higher than his belt buckle!), but at his worst H is a skirt chaser and is always and forever looking for the bigger, better deal (or trophy woman).

Cro-Magnon (C). The final edition to the evolutionary foursome, C is designated **homo sapiens**, the "thinking man." He is the wise one, the leader of the pack, and the master of the disguise. C has learned to master multiple roles yet can be fulfilling on many levels. But beware, with this complexity comes a need to explore and move up and onward. C is on a quest. He understands that the highest expression of man is **service** to "man's kind" (as our friend Howard always calls us) and he is out to find his place in that servitude. C is purposeful in a different way from his brothers. What's more, he can talk about it, philosophize about it, and write about it. C has created these tools—not for the tools themselves, but as a means to the ends of service. Be careful; talk is not to be confused with action. C needs to have commitment to complete the package. Sexually, he is a lover who focuses on you. This man has a huge heart and you will feel taken care of and have companionship with this him, so long as you ask for what you want. Spiritually he is deeply devout but rarely finds that outlet in formal religion. Once he stops talking and gets into action, he is a hero, but quite often, we have to tell him to stop talking so much. As a result of his humanitarian side, C may never make much money. At his best, C makes dreams come true. He shines with saintly luminance and makes a genuine difference in the world. At his worst, he is all air, all talk, and great ideas. As a mate, you would do well to ask him each day what his commitment is. Just keep him putting one foot in front of the other.

These are our men—yeah, they're ours. As men, we love them all, each with his contributions and foibles. Together we make a team. And if you ask us which is more evolved or better, or which will make a more suitable mate, we'll most likely say we have no idea. We all have our faults and all have our great points. Underneath it all, none is much more advanced than our cave-dwelling ancestors. What you don't understand about us is that the unconditional love of a good woman will transform any of these types into the finest of his kind, bringing out his best characteristics.[3]

We wrote this guide for all men. We did not and will not assume that some are better able than others to understand our content. We wrote this at the basic, common level that all brothers, men, jerks, and other blokes on the bus of life can understand. We are men, nothing more, but certainly nothing less! We actually say—out loud, in public—that we love men. And we hope that you are reading this book because you love them too.

That is the last thing we will say actually directed to you women. You are welcome to listen in on our conversation with our brothers, but don't expect that it makes sense in "women's terms." As Armstrong says, we are not just "hairy women."[4] We don't think like women, talk like women, or have a valuing system like women. As we said at the beginning of this section, we will be speaking the language of men talking with men, so if that makes sense to you—welcome in, if not, hand this back to your husband!

---

3 You might serve yourself well by reading *Making Sense of Men* by Alison A. Armstrong who can give you some very valuable hints on how to bring out the very best in your man.

4 Alison A. Armstrong, *Making Sense of Men, A Woman's Guide to a Lifetime of Love, Care and Attention from All Men,* PAX Programs, Inc., Sherman Oaks, CA, 2007, p. 12.

WE KNOW WOMEN!

> *"I have worshipped woman as the living embodiment*
> *of the spirit of service and sacrifice."*
> **Mahatma Gandhi**

> *"Let men tremble to win the hand of woman, unless they*
> *win along with it the utmost passion of her heart!"*
> **Nathaniel Hawthorne**

On our bad days, we like to believe that we know women. On our worst days, we also want others to think that we know women and what they want and like. However, on our good days, we both admit that we haven't a clue; that after a couple of decades of successful married life (each) we haven't figured women out. It's the truth, Bucko—we haven't! We are not purporting to know women. It would neither be prudent to make that assertion nor would it make any logical sense. We are both men—heterosexual men in long-term, committed, monogamous marriage relationships—and what we actually "know" about women could fit in a thimble. But what we can report to you, from our experiences and from those of the many, many men who we have helped to stay in their committed relationships, is **what works from the man's side of the equation.**

There are a few places in this book, however, where it's necessary to explain something about how women are (from our perspective) in order to help you avoid some common pitfalls. We've used our own observations about women, as well as the collected wisdom of others with whom we agree. The section called "Women are Different" is an example of such folk wisdom. But remember, the biggest pitfall is believing that you really know much about women at all. So take it with a grain of salt!

Now, our wives told both of us after they read the book that we were talking out of our rear orifices and had missed the mark when it comes to understanding them and other women. Moreover, sources very close to us have said, in as many words, "Women don't like men who think they know women!" That's cool, as it is not our intent to increase our likeability to women, with the possible exceptions of our wives. We freely admit that, like Chance in Jerzy Kosinski's *Being There*, whose assumptions about courtship and relationship came entirely from watching TV, we have only half the story. Our intent is simply to tell you only what you really need to know about women. We'll let John Gray[5] or somebody like that give you the definitive version—though we might suggest a female author like Gray's former wife, Barbara DeAngelis.[6]

---

5 John Gray, *Men Are From Mars, Women Are From Venus*, HarperCollins, New York, NY, 1992. Though there are at least a dozen more in the Mars and Venus series, this was the foundation of them all. For a more complete reference list, see the resources section at the end of this guide.

6 Barbara DeAngelis, *What Women Want Men to Know: the Ultimate Book about Love, Sex, and Relationships for You*, Hyperion, New York, NY, 2001

Despite all of those caveats, our assertions, assumptions, and characterizations about women have, over time, proven to help other men in explaining some of the "mystery" of the female mystique. The bottom line is this book is a compilation of tips and advice collected from men for men concerning what works as men in relationships with women.

WE LOVE WOMEN

W

e need to comment on our point of view in writing this book. There is an undercurrent in us (and we assume with many men) that appears to be an animosity toward women. It is not that we (Dave and Kris) think that women are bad or evil or diseased in some way. Rather it stems, we believe, from a long history of not getting what we want when we want it. Women alter our paths, which, as men, we would prefer to be straight as an arrow. When we have to duck and weave and bob, it annoys us. It is natural—not bad, just natural. Similarly, women are reported to have a distrust and often a fear of men—not bad, just what is.

Lest you think that we have a negative view of women or of our wives, let us get this straight. We firmly believe that:

o   Our women and women in general are the most fantastic creatures ever created.

o   We want to enjoy the benefits of being in relationships with our women for a significantly long period.

o   We are interested in, committed to, and actively engaged in regularly helping others of our gender achieve long-lasting, monogamous, and successful marriages.

It is precisely because of those reasons that we are writing this guide. This is our survival guide as well as yours. We offer these tips from experiences in what works and what does not work in maintaining the glue that holds marriages together.

> *Survival Tip:* Never assume that you fully know your woman or any women, for that matter. The moment you assume that—as the saying goes—you'll make an ass out of you and me (ass-u-me).

SECTION 2

GETTING YOUR BEARINGS

"You can't control anything except your commitment to it."
Andrew Young

Without a compass to guide you through the wilderness, you will end up lost and walking is circles. Without mentors to guide you through the terrain of marriage, you can get deeply lost—you can even lose your self. This section deals with those essential tools you need to navigate the path ahead.

(Kris and Dave)

DISCIPLINE

> *"Strength does not come from physical capacity. It comes*
> *from an indomitable will."*
> **Mahatma Gandhi**

B eing in relationship is a discipline. It takes work and practice.
You have to be paying attention to it (the relationship itself)
or it will starve a slow death. You have to be awake and
aware all the time, making sure you are giving your absolute best to
it. And when you know, we mean really know, that you are giving
your absolute best to it, no matter how it looks in the moment, you
will feel a fulfillment and sense of accomplishment that can have
you conquer the world. But it will take Olympian discipline.

The dictionary defines the noun version of discipline in many
ways:

o   It is a field of study (and by all means you must take this
    on as a field of study). You need to study your mate and
    you must study your behavior in relationship with her—
    what you *actually* do, not what you *intended* to do. Ask your-

self, "How am I showing up in this relationship—for my woman?"

o It is a training that "corrects, molds or perfects" your being. How you should take on being in this relationship is as a training modality. Your wife and the demands of the relationship will be the best (or worst—depending on how you view these things) drill instructor and coach you will ever have. You must submit to this training and be shaped and molded into a better, more powerful man by it. And the training never stops.

o It is the control or orderly conduct gained by obedience to the laws and rules. Ouch! That one stings! Being disciplined and following this training rigorously will result in your ability to control yourself and live within the realm of the relationship. Men are, by design, loners and undisciplined, according to most male writers.[7] In order to fit ourselves into the proper space in the relationship and not blow it up or shoot ourselves in the foot, we need to be disciplined—in every sense and meaning of the word.

o And, as if that were not enough, the dictionary provides us with discipline as a verb: to punish or penalize in order to train, control, or correct. Double ouch! In other words, we either adopt the discipline or the failure to do so will result in a "penalty," the pain of which will serve to correct our behavior. Living in a relationship either takes or provides the discipline!

> There can be no back door to marriage but if I create one, I close it.

What forces that discipline on us is being in this monogamous relationship "for as long as we both shall live." Making that

---

7 See the resources section. In particular, Robert Bly, Richard Rohr, and other classical writers about the male experience reference our need for freedom from rules and constraints as our basic undisciplined selves. The "wild man" must be trained.

commitment does something very scary to a man: it effectively shuts the backdoor escape route from the relationship (should you think one day that you just can't take it anymore). You choose to shut the door, padlock it, weld it in place, brick it over, and then plaster and paint it so that there is no memory of any door ever being there! *When you are inescapably confined in this relationship with no possible exit, you are forced to learn the discipline of relationship—which includes the imperative to work out whatever it is that makes you want to leave.* Single men (and we all were single at one time) have the possibility of escape. If their girlfriends become too problematic or high maintenance, well, as Paul Simon says, "there must be fifty ways to leave." But if you are married or intending to be married, you will have to close off that escape route and learn to become disciplined.

This may be the first of those points where you may start thinking that this is not a fun book. You may be entertaining one of two thoughts.

This is a very scary proposition for some men, and this may be a point where you start thinking that we are crazy and painting a picture of doom, that we don't know what we're talking about or are overstating our point, and that perhaps the rest of this book is going to be a waste of your time. If you are thinking this, you are probably in the majority of men on this planet. You may be doubtful about anything that sounds like self-help or pop psychology. But we're betting that a part of you is whispering that we're on to something here. You realize (as we do) that as men we are fucked when it comes to relationships. And we mean *totally* fucked, because in our core we don't really care about relationship, and we have not been schooled in relationship skills.

Everybody has difficulties and the details will make it look like it is the first time anyone ever had this and it is not. When it happens you need to recognize that you need help and that cannot be you – ask for help and there is no shame in the admission of failure.

But maybe also you get it—because you are awake in this curious, inexplicable, and foreign situation called marriage. You realize that you have signed up for the journey and that you will need all the help you can get in surviving it. This journey is the kind of adventure you read about in books. It is just like your favorite DVD in your collection.

It is the movie you will keep watching over and over again, with scenes like the one that grabs you in the guts at the end of *Saving Private Ryan*—where Tom Hanks whispers "Earn this!" It is a story full of action, drama, and comedy. You don't know where it will turn next, but you keep watching the movie because you know you have to. And because you know you want to. And you don't want the story to be a tragedy, so you know you need help. Well, we're right there with you, man—we needed help too, and we still do. The next section is about finding that help.

Survival Tip: Notice where you lack discipline in your relationship with your wife—some behavior or area of neglect that you want to change. Adopt a daily discipline aimed at turning this around.

LEARNING FROM MEN AND MENTORS

"Knowledge speaks, but wisdom listens."
Jimi Hendrix

O nly men can teach the lessons contained in this guide. Men and women think differently, a fact which, despite all feminist protestations, is well substantiated by a vast amount of psychological research. Rohr writes, "I am convinced that there is a 'male' way of feeling [and a] male way of thinking. But women cannot teach us...we need a man to do that for us."[8] What you learn from male mentors will make more sense to you as a man than any coaching we could get from a woman. Now, you may think that there may, in fact, be elements of this domain (that of being married to and staying fully engaged with one specific woman) that might best come from a woman, but this guide is not about

---

8 Richard Rohr, *Wild Man to Wise Man, Reflections in Male Spirituality*, Cincinnati OH, St. Anthony Messenger Press, 2005, p. 81.

understanding the female mind.[9] How could a woman know what a man must do to be a successful husband? She may know what she wants from a husband, but there is much more to being a successful husband than satisfying her wishes.

Learning from men is a trip! Men do what we like to refer to as "inflicting love" on each other. Our methods are a little less than smooth, shall we say. An elder was once teaching about the art of being present and, as I was sitting next to him, he casually asked me to give him my hand—which, of course, I did. Without hesitating he took my hand up to his mouth and bit my index finger so hard that I screamed out and was certain I'd see blood. And then, just as casually, he asked, "Now when I bit your finger, could you think of anything else? That's what I mean by being present!" Often, good lessons come on the other side of a figurative smack across the head with a big stick (or a literal bite of the finger!). Men teach men differently than schoolteachers (most of whom are women) do.

If you already have a men's team or a circle of men you teach and learn from (not just your bowling league), or are looking for one, make certain that it includes successfully married men. Men who have fifteen or more years of successful marriage—in the same relationship—probably have figured something out and at least have outlived some of their greater crashes. It will do you no good—and will most likely cause you great harm—to take advice from single or divorced men on how to live in a committed relationship with a woman. They may have opinions on the subject, but just thank them for sharing and move on—what they have to say is of no value to you. *They do not know what they are talking about.* Would you take financial advice from a penniless bum? Then don't take marriage advice from single men. It is that simple.

---

9 For an excellent treatise on that subject read *The Female Brain*, by Louann Brizendine, Broadway Books, New York, NY, 2006).

You should also make sure that there are wise elders in your men's circle. The first half of a man's life journey deals with defining oneself by duties, victories, accomplishments, and the accumulation of wealth and goods.[10] That may be sufficient for getting you into a marriage— many psychologists report that women tend to seek out successful men more than simply good-looking men—but it will not be sufficient to sustain you in that place. The second half of the journey is one of gaining wisdom by letting go of the stuff you have collected in life. The wisdom journey recognizes wounds, not victories, as the greatest teachers, and older men will have accumulated certain wisdom courtesy of those wounds, battles, and past pains. Seek out wizened men whose compassion for your desire to succeed in marriage comes from knowing the pains of having taken several arrows straight in the chest. They have experienced what it is to fail and to recover without losing the entire relationship. They know the great fact of successful relationships: success is being able to stay married despite your differences, despite the arguments, and despite all the "fuck you's" that would sink most weaker relationships or marriages of convenience.

Another caution: popular opinion is as dangerous as advice from women and single men, so beware of men spouting platitudes and generalities that don't come from their own experience. As Rohr states, "What we call reality, and what we are almost totally addicted to, is largely a construct of men who frankly have not worked much on their inner lives."[11] A man who has leaned into and learned from the resistance his wife has provided has been forced to do the inner work.

But men are not all the same. We live out of what many call "archetypes." Archetypes are patterns or classical ways of being that have been common among men and women throughout the ages. Though there are many male archetypes, most writers agree on four main

---

10 Rohr, *Wild Man*, 2007, p. 192.

11 Rohr, *Wild Man*, p. 9.

masculine roles: The Warrior, The Lover, The King, and The Magician.[12] Each of these male roles will play out differently in relationship, each has a major lesson to learn, and from a mentoring perspective, each has a distinct lesson to teach other men. Furthermore, you may shift through several or all of them on your journey through life. So, early in life you may be the Warrior and, after you have gotten the lesson, shift to King and ultimately to Magician/Wise Man.

It is the perils and tests in life that challenge and form us, and ultimately develop and mature us and help us move on. Each archetype has its own set of challenges, tests, and lessons. To address how you might face some of the challenges, we offer our adaptation of the Moore and Gillette interpretation, proffered from our years of living those truths.

The Warrior—As boys and young men we enter life instinctively knowing how to fight. It is in our genes. Men glorify the so-called warriors, the gladiators, and the super athletes. We think the fight makes the Warriors sacred idols. So our lesson in this realm is learning that fighting is *not* the gift of the Warrior. But the Warrior, through countless battles, painful wounds and the scars they leave behind, learns that becoming powerful means knowing *which* battles are worth fighting and that it is not necessary to fight to the death over every little thing. For the transformation of Warrior—from the fighter to protector—he must learn what is sacred and worth standing guard over, taking the blows, the arrows, and the perpetual onslaught of attack without yielding.

The Warrior is the rescuer of damsels in distress. He will likely choose for a wife a woman who needs rescuing, and in the early years of marriage, he is busy slaying dragons for his fair maiden.

---

12 The classic text on this subject is by Robert Moore and Douglas Gillette entitled, appropriately, *Warrior, King, Lover, Magician*, Harper Collins, New York, NY, 1990. It should be a standard in any man's collection.

But there may come a time when she grows beyond the need for rescue, and then she is no longer the woman he once wanted or needed. The danger that a Warrior faces in marriage is not being able to adapt to this change in his woman (though there may also be cases where his damsel will never change and consume all his time, always needing to be rescued). In either case, the lesson he must learn is how to be the silent protector for her as she risks and tries out new roles, activities, and ways of being. He must surrender his sword, and stand down. He must become her safe haven so she can venture out and blossom.

The Lover—Every boy is Prince Charming and every young man fancies himself to be a Casanova. The Lover archetype is lust masquerading as a would-be father. Early in life, the Lover treats love as a series of conquests, collecting notches on his belt. He lusts for the dark, moist, inner cave of a woman as if it will mystically give him something—some life secret. He somehow feels that the passion of orgasm is a birth/death/rebirth transformation. Because he loses himself in that moment of ecstasy, he is drawn into believing that sex is somehow meaningful and transformative. But in truth, the uninitiated Lover is a narcissist, seeking in his "soul mate" only his own completion. In this quest partner after partner mortally wounds him, and he may conclude that he can't bear to take that risk of vulnerability again. Or he may, if he's alert, be transformed from the Lover who plays at co-creating birth to one who makes the supreme sacrifice of death. The gift of the Lover is to lay down his life for another, to love so fully and completely that his life is given up as a sacrifice—as he lets his ego and self completely die. When his ego dies to that truth, he becomes love; he is the ultimate Lover.

Marriage for the Lover moves from fantasy and narcissism to an emancipating love. The shift in attention is totally away from him to her. When loving and sex are no longer about getting, when there is no longer a need for even orgasm, the Lover has made the transition. However, the Lover must not lose *himself* in the transition.

In many ways, we are all Lovers. We all must learn that life is not about us. Ultimately, you and I are not important. As a man, your life is not yours; rather, god/universe is living out its purpose through you, and through that purpose, you are in service to others. When your ego dies to that truth, you become love, you *ARE* the ultimate Lover.

The King—Men are born to be Kings, and from early childhood, they play at King games (King of the Hill). Men want to be in charge, longing for ultimate power, yet feel the stinging truth of their absolute powerlessness. The transformation for King is from powerful lord to giver—from amassing wealth to giving it all away and bestowing as much as possible to others, benevolently and humbly. To do this, the King must learn grace and humility; however, this abrupt about-face comes with a price tag. At some point, the King recognizes the responsibility that has come with the victories he has won. What at first seemed like the privilege of dominion over the land and its people transforms before his eyes into responsibility for the well-being of both. When he is strong and well, his people prosper; when he stumbles and falls, they suffer. The King must be able to name that weighted moment when, as a ruler, he took responsibility and gave up everything in order to sustain and enrich his people—that is, his family, his team, his company, or whatever group is primary to him. Then and only then can he truly understand the servant-leader's life.

The King is every woman's fantasy mate. Much of the stuff of fairy tales and fables is about the Prince becoming the King and his Lady becoming the Queen. When the shift from lord of all to servant comes, it may look to the King's partner like betrayal and abandonment. After all, many women desire the power of being

Queen and the comfort of the throne and palace. It is most important that the King take his Queen with him on the servant journey, appealing to her motherly and caring nature.

The Magician—The Magician is the keeper of "withheld mysteries." What makes a David Copperfield or a Criss Angel great is that neither reveals the trick behind the illusion. Transformation for the Magician is from one who uses illusion and confusion to get his way, to the Sage who reveals the hidden truth of the universe for the benefit of all. This is often the final transformation for most Elders and perhaps the toughest lesson, for he can no longer pretend not to know the truth about our life, the lives of all we meet, and most importantly, the commonality we share with all other men. The energy of the Magician takes many forms: from the Trickster and Jester in his younger years to the Healer and Medicine Man later in life. Regardless of the form it takes, the Magician role trains the eye. Through this training, the Magician begins to see truth from all angles and eventually learns to discern the inner truth of the world. It is the knowing without knowing why or how that comes to fruition. The world may have seemed to be covert, illusive, and underhanded, but the Magician finally learns to see beneath the surface. Like so many of the male lessons, this one is hard-won. More often than not, the "seeing" comes only after a severe two-by-four to the head of his logic and belief systems.

This is the ultimate "Wild Man to Wise Man" transition, as Richard Rohr calls it, and it may present some problems in a marriage. The Jester who has become a Wise Man must acknowledge that his woman originally chose him for his lightness of being (possibly because of her own seriousness and heaviness). The Wise Man must not ever take himself too seriously! The true Sage sees the humor in life's paradoxes and illusions, and he uses his jokes and tricks to enlighten and teach, rather than to elevate himself. And, when he learns to bring his wife with him on this journey, theirs is a joint path even greater than that of the benevolent King and Queen, as they teach the wisdom of relationships to the next generation.

A note of caution: as the Jester matures into the Wise Man, he may find a sage woman waiting to join him. However having two serious heavyweights in the house can be nearly lethal. Someone will have to be able to laugh!

The archetypes, in other words, are just a method to describe some of the common ways we men live life. It may not be an exact science but if you take it generically, there is some wisdom in there. It is not perfect—just another angle shot. You will most likely fit into one of these four archetypes as will your mentors. So let us turn briefly to them.

Choosing Mentors. Let us now turn to getting the kind of training to become a successful married adult male that will be of some assistance in your journey ahead. Mentors provide that guidance and training. To navigate this passage we need mentors, guides who have walked down the path ahead of us and who know what it takes to survive. Mentoring is not "nice," nor is it "fun." So it is important to know which path you are on and to know where you are on that path. And it is important to be able to recognize the archetype of your mentor. There are advantages and disadvantages in choosing a mentor who is on the same archetypal path as you are. Chose wisely! As we have said, each type has a distinct set of lessons learned from living out that archetype. However, as you listen to their advice, be aware of the lens and filter through which the man has seen and is seeing the world. Is it wise to get love advice from a Lover? Is the King the best source of wisdom on how to run a home? There is no rule about who you must choose. Each has his gift and each has his blind spot. But if you choose a "nice" mentor, you may never get the lessons you need and require.

The Warrior Mentor. The Warrior has learned the gift that other men are in his life—they are his platoon, his squad, his safety net. He started out alone, sword (or weapon of choice) in hand, but found that there were others on this path and that they all stood a better chance of survival collectively. Together they readied each other for the battles, and they called out the bullshit that men so often tell themselves. Warrior Mentors know the value of being able to trust your men, and of when to go to them for what you need. This type of mentor will serve you well as an advisor on truth and commitment. Mahatma Gandhi (believe it or not—he was a formidable, though nonviolent, Warrior) was an excellent example of this type of mentoring.

The Lover Mentor. The Lover will see you for your true self. Having grown out of his inborn narcissism, he is keen on sniffing out the self-serving and needy attitudes of other men. Because he paid the price of self-centeredness, he can see it easily in other men. His gentle but stern warning should be taken in, but you need to listen carefully, because the Lover will not speak with the same power as the Warrior that hits like the full frontal attack of a Sumo Wrestler. Don't be fooled by his quiet demeanor; the Lover is a stern teacher, and can show you the deep cuts you could experience if you do not heed his warning. Jesus of Nazareth was the ultimate Lover Mentor.

The King Mentor. Men most frequently seek out the King for his wise counsel. His lordly wisdom and his sense of certainty lend a level of power to his points. But care should be taken here because the King mentor must be willing to show you the dark side of his frailty, and the pain of his having decided too

> I know which men to call when I need to just bitch. These men know how great a husband I am so they listen for me to be great. My ego drops and I am able to give my wife the love she deserves.

soon. Unless you hear his burden, the man you are talking to has not fully matured into his wisdom and is just dispensing advice. But one who knows the burden of carrying the needs of his people, who has suffered with them, will be able to lead you to your own grounded certainty. Nelson Mandela is a great example of the King Mentor.

The Magician Mentor. Conversely, no one wants to hear the advice and counsel of the Wizard! His is a jagged little pill at best, and a truth that is hard to swallow. Moreover, the Wizard/Magician often teaches with paradox and parables that are puzzling and disquieting. If you can get past these, the wisdom he dispenses will catapult you forward into a new dimension. The Magician and Wizard offer transformation—but to get there you may have to walk through the darkest night your soul could ever imagine! Siddhartha Gautama stands as the exemplar of Magician Mentor.

Mentors provide the last part of the fathering we all are missing from the time we left (or he left us). Rohr, who runs a center and training for mentoring men (called M.A.L.E.s—Men As Leaders and Elders) says that most of men grow up with an emptiness inside that he calls "father hunger." Unless another man—a mentor— takes us through that completion, the emptiness turns inwardly to become depression or outwardly to become rage and anger. Neither will serve you in your marriage. Get a mentor, sit down, shut up, and listen to him!

The Core of Masculinity (a short poem on mentors by the thirteenth-century Sufi poet, Rumi)[13]

> The core of masculinity does not derive
> from being male,
> nor friendliness from those who console.
> Your old grandmother says, "Maybe you shouldn't
> go to school. You look a little pale."
> Run when you hear that.
> A father's stern slaps are better.
> Your bodily soul wants comforting.
> The severe father wants spiritual clarity.
> He scolds but eventually
> leads you into the open.
> Pray for a tough instructor
> to hear and act and stay within you.
> We have been busy accumulating solace.
> Make us afraid of how we were.

Survival Tip: Pick out the most intimidating, infuriating, and exasperating man you know. Look at him through the lens of a student and discover what he has been trying to teach you. Extra credit: Forge a relationship with him and keep learning.

---

13 Rumi (translation by Coleman Barks), in *The Rag and Bone Shop of the Heart, Poems for Men*, by Robert Bly, James Hillman and Michael Meade, Harper Perennial, New York, NY, 1992, p. 135.

GROWTH AND DEVELOPMENT

"Everything that irritates us about others can lead us to an
understanding of ourselves."

Carl Jung

What we are really talking about here is your growth and development. How do things develop? How has natural selection worked throughout the ages? Species change and morph because they *have* to, when the way that they are just doesn't work anymore. On an evolutionary level, the maxim is "grow or die."

How do you adapt and grow as an individual? The same way—when what you are doing or how you are being doesn't work anymore, you have to change. As you look back on your own life, you will probably notice that you have learned far more from life's setbacks than you did from your successes. In fact, people learn little or nothing from success except that whatever they just did must have worked. A good example is the MLB hitter who goes up to the plate and taps his shoes, just to get the dirt off his spikes, then quite coincidentally follows it up by smacking a homer. So guess what—his brain puts those things together (tap shoes, hit homer), and he decides to try it again. The pattern puts him in a kind of "zone" state and the next time he taps his shoes—surprise—he gets another hit, maybe even a home run! And so the patterns are iced in. But people rarely learn anything useful from success.

Failures are another story. Our greatest life lessons have always been on the heels of great disasters. "OW! Well, I really learned a heap from that!" or "Note to self, don't do that again!" The truth is that we will NOT really grow and develop into maturity *until and unless* we are sufficiently uncomfortable, sufficiently in pain, or sufficiently out of our element. No pain, no gain! It is a process of breakdown and breakthrough. A way of being has to fail, break down, or die before you can learn a new life lesson. You just can't hear the new lesson until the old beliefs and structures get out of the way. As Albert Einstein famously said, "No problem can be solved from the same level of consciousness that created it." In other words, what got you here won't get you there. That old belief, that old skill, that old way of being will not work any longer and must die. And some will not go quietly! It may take a keg of dynamite to blast you into the next level.

In that sense, marriage will most certainly develop you, but only if it is your intention that it do so. Men who refuse to let marriage be their teacher usually end up divorced (or dead from a heart attack). Later on we will discuss how it is your woman's job and nature to test you and accelerate your growth and development, but for now, just know that you are in the middle of the biggest and best developmental experience you may ever get.

If you signed up for marriage to have the comfy life, to enjoy good, safe, steady sex from a Stepford wife, we are afraid we have little or no wisdom to share with you. Please donate this book to another man who is not living in a fantasy world and enjoy yours while you have it—we envy you and wish you well.

So if you can deal with our insulting you (hey, men do that), you are definitely one of us on this incredible trip. Now hang on, because we have many more obstacles to surmount before we are finished. So let's plow forward.

MEN AND POWER

"If a man prioritizes his relationship over his highest purpose, he weakens himself, disserves the universe, and cheats his woman of an authentic man who can offer her full, undivided presence."

David Deida

You are powerful far beyond your superhero comic book fantasy! As a man, you are most likely more physically powerful than your woman partner. Though a friend of ours was nicknamed "the man with a larger wife" by his host tribe back in the Peace Corps days, most of us are not only slightly taller but our physiology and athleticism are usually greater. So, irrespective and quite apart from the reference to woman-power we make in discussing *their* superhuman powers (see the discussion in section 4 called "Women are Different"), in physical battle we most often would come out the victor. This little fact has some serious implications.

Your strength and power are part of what attracted her to you in the first place (in addition to your good looks, great sense of humor, and superior intelligence, of course). Later on we will discuss how there is a "Little Girl" aspect to your woman who still wants to hold on to Daddy's hand and be safe. This comes from women's ancient genetic programming that senses their innate vulnerability in pregnancy and childbirth, and demands protection. But there is a raw, almost sexual attraction to that strength as well. Just as we men drool over women with big breasts and a wide pelvic spread, many women want a man with a Schwarzenegger build to be "their man." We have our "trophy wives" and they have their "trophy husbands." It is a delight, they say, to walk into the party holding on to a stud. The dream of being "swept off their feet" or carried across the threshold of their new house still lives in the deeper recesses of the female psyche—however dull or faintly it exists. Your strength is attractive.

But this sword called strength cuts two ways—a man's physical power is protective, but it's also dangerous. Be careful! You are a killer at heart. There is a rapist in your soul. Men have evolved over eons to be killers and rapists. Think about it: our history is one of war and conquest, and who do you think survived those battles—the nice guys? Hell, no! It was the killer—the Viking, the Hun, and the Visigoth—who laid waste to the villages and dragged the women off as their prize! Throughout history, there have been few generations of men whose ranks have not been thinned out by the hand of war and death, leaving only the winners and more alpha males as the generators of the seed for their successors. Even "civilized" men hold the fantasy that they, like Rhett Butler, can kiss the protesting Scarlet into submission. That, my friend, is rape! You have inherited that genetic predisposition to kill, rape, and take what you want, and your woman is quite aware—also at the chromosomal level—of that truth.

So it's not surprising that at the same time a woman is attracted to her man's power, she feels vulnerable and fears it. She feels like she could be a victim of that power at any time, and has a fear of her husband in the background, even if he never lays a hand on her or raises his voice. Kris' wife explained this once. She was counseling a woman on the phone and when she got off, she said that the woman felt like "prey" around her husband. When Kris questioned the use of that particular word, she replied that "all women feel like prey." The concept floored him—having, at six three and 235 lb., never felt like prey—but even a buddy of ours who is five six says the same thing. We never realized how different the experience of a woman was until then.

When we really thought about it, it made sense. Girls grow up being ogled and whistled at, groped and objectified. Date rape is a fairly regular occurrence that is probably not reported even half as much as it happens. Something like one in three women over the age of twenty-one has been the victim of sexual abuse or rape. There have probably been times when your woman—even in the confines of marriage—has felt she had to give in and let you have her. And being naked, legs spread apart, and having some-one—some stronger, harder entity—physically penetrate her soft and open body must indeed feel vulnerable in ways men cannot even imagine. Different women experience these feelings to different degrees, but it's not difficult to understand why they are there for all women.

In spite of that, women still select one of their predators and marry him! When they wake up to that, they realize they are, in some respect, indeed sleeping with the enemy. So all of that strength you offer may never take away the core fear that so many women live with. Don't get mad at her when she tells you that, even though she is walking beside you, she is scared in a bad neighborhood, or, though in the same room with you, she says she can't sleep on the ground floor with the slider open.

And beyond your ability to violate her body—beyond your killer nature—you also have the power to crush your wife's spirit. Your woman is like a flower (yeah, really!), and you can crush her in the most simple and subtle ways. She needs to thrive in womanly ways that you will never be able to provide; she needs to go to those places that nourish her feminine soul—and you need to get over the fact that these places are outside of you! She may want to take up drumming in a Gaia circle or do some artsy thing that makes you cringe ("seriously, honey—wanna scrapbook with me?"). Don't resist, don't criticize, don't even roll your eyes. You will be the beneficiary—she will come back to you more alive and juicy and attractive than ever.

You can crush her spirit in other ways too: simply deny her opinion by never asking for it (we men are notorious for not asking for help); don't value anything she does; invalidate her choice of clothing and hairstyle by not even noticing; tell her that your mom cooked eggs better than she does; make a passing comment on her stretch marks; criticize her choice of curtains or color décor in the house. Any of these sound familiar? Can you think of any others that you do (or don't do)?

Your job is to praise your woman, to delight in her choices—don't just pretend to, but really delight in them because they are a reflection of the woman you love. Remember that what you hold in your power is the ability to snuff out that beautiful flame in a heartbeat, or to fuel it so that it shines brighter.

> You need to call Triple A roadside assistance for marriage help: appreciation, acknowledgement and admiration.

All of the times you use your power to hurt, cause harm, or otherwise threaten the safety of this fragile and easily overpowered female you call your wife will be stored in a "safety file"—a memory of incidents and evidence to which she can refer in regularly evaluating her sense of safety with you. We will say more about the list of hurts in her safety file memory bank later on in the section on "Trust."

And finally, possibly the worst way you can hurt your wife is to treat her like a man—your wife is *NOT* a man! If you get too comfortable in your relationship, you may forget this simple fact (after all, isn't there at least a tiny part of you that wishes you could have a buddy for a roommate and a maid and a concubine instead of a wife?). As soon as you do, you are on the slippery slope of doom that can end up in a dead relationship, in a mundane life, or in her looking for nourishment elsewhere. Remember how, when you courted her, there wasn't a thing she did that didn't turn you on? You probably even liked her burps and farts and thought they were cute and adorable! And when you stop adoring her, she will eventually seek that adoration elsewhere, not realizing that what-ever man she meets will court her in the same way, only to forget those behaviors in the next phase of the relationship (unless he has read this book, of course!). You need to continually court her, to be the man she would be tempted to have an affair with, the man she would cheat on *you* for![14]

This section about the use and abuse of your power is not just a list of dos and don'ts. It goes deeper than that—you have to really feel and own your power. And when you do, it will be easy to see where you are on the right path and where you are heading toward a dead end or a cliff. But you can't do it alone—you need your men and a mentor: first, to help you step into your power in a balanced way; second, to let them know where you are and where you want to go; and third, to get the help that only a men's circle can provide.

---

14 Wayne M. Levine, *Hold On To Your N.U.T.s, The Relationship Manual For Men*, BetterMen Press, Austin, TX, 2007, p. 113

Survival Tip: Find the killer in you and get to know him. Denying that he is part of your being will inevitably result in his manifesting at the worst time. Not knowing your killer is not being in control.

On Not Being an Asshole

Consultant Robert Sutton did the working world a huge favor by finally speaking the unspeakable in his book *The No Asshole Rule*.[15] While written about jerks and assholes of the working world, his concepts apply equally in marriage and we won't try to summarize all of the attributes associated with being an asshole here. But in the chapter on stopping your inner jerk, Sutton has some helpful tips.[16]

If you look in the mirror and know that despite your best efforts there are days and times when, plain and simple, you are being an asshole to your wife, recognize along with that how very contagious being an asshole is. As we always say, "The problem with assholes is that everyone has one." So not too surprisingly, when your inner asshole rears up, it's an invitation to hers to join the party. Just don't go there.

---

15 Robert I Sutton, *The No Asshole Rule, Building a Civilized Workplace and Surviving One That Isn't*, Warner Business Books, New York, NY, 2007.

16 Sutton, *No Asshole*, p. 95ff.

As a man, you are by nature competitive and competitions have winners and losers. When you set up for win/lose, you are becoming a relationship asshole. Sutton suggests that the easiest thing to do is use first person plural more in your speaking—"we" not "I." Your wife will appreciate that, as it automatically takes it out of competition and places it in win/win partnership.

Additionally, we males are hierarchical—we see things in more-than and less-than. We are always comparing (from the time you noticed that your dick was bigger or smaller than the kid at the next urinal). We're not saying that you have to believe that men and women are the same, but you must not compare her to yourself or anyone else: her profession (yes, housewife is a profession), how much money she makes, how hard she works, etc. That is being a Class A asshole!

If you find yourself recognizing some of these as yours, then take a page from AA, Sutton suggests. Admitting that you are an asshole (even at times) is the first step to recovery. And personally, we are both big fans of the lessons and processes outlined in the twelve-step process. We don't know if there is an Assholes Anonymous, but if there is, we might go looking for a sponsor and start hitting meetings!

The No Asshole Rule wraps up the Jerk chapter with a handy little self-assessment (which we were embarrassed when taking). Do your wife a favor, pick up Sutton's book, turn to the test on pages 124–126 and then act accordingly!

> *Survival Tip:* Get the small pocket version of the little blue Alcoholics Anonymous book—it's five dollars very well spent—and just follow through the process, substituting asshole for alcoholic.

"Balanced" Masculinity

*"As a body in a world, here is our choice: we can be more
loving or less loving. That's it."*
David Deida

There is a popular myth about men needing to "embrace
their feminine side" in order to be balanced in a relationship. We suggest that this is the echo of the feminist movement of the sixties and seventies. During that time, as women took
the stage and claimed their rights to be humans of equal stature
to their male counterparts (rightly so), it somehow became more
than unfashionable to be masculine. It became evil and wrong, and
as a result, most men became feminized. Those who refused, or
couldn't become Sensitive New-Age Guys (we call them SNAGs),
were labeled Neanderthals and Cretans. I remember once being
told that I must sit when I spoke with women so that I wouldn't
come across as domineering.

But there is something missing in this discussion. We humans were made male and female by our Creator (or by grand design, evolution, or whatever you want to believe). We are males, through and through, and we do not have to pretend for a moment that we have some feminine aspects in order to be a balanced and healthy member of a relationship.

The proof is right in front of you. Take a look at your genitals. There are two elements to male sexuality: one—the one we unfortunately tend to be over balance toward—is protruding, up, and hard. The penis is the essence of what many think it means to be male. This essence is like a heat-seeking missile, homing in on targets in the world and thrusting into them. It is strong, hard, and powerful when in missile mode, and, lest we forget, flaccid when not. But there is another part to your genitalia—just behind the power unit is a soft sac containing your most vulnerable element—the testes. Your testicles are the essence of creativity, and partnering with the female's ovaries, the source of life. Our female counterparts tend to forget that fact (and may want us to forget it too), since they carry the result of our life-creating element. But with all their life-giving power, the testicles are quite soft, tender, and in need of protection.

Men tend to see only their tough side and forget that they have this tenderness and natural vulnerability—until they get a kick in the groin! If you have had that life-altering experience, you know the sick-in-the-gut feeling of not taking care to protect your vulnerability. So you need to remember this: you are hard AND soft, giving AND receiving, penetrating AND able to be deeply wounded—and NONE of that is feminine. Masculinity is all of that, and you need to accept that about yourself before you can gain balance as a man.

Too much "dick" and you become a violent conqueror; a virtual rapist loose in the world (maybe that's why men use "dickhead" as an insult!). You will seek and destroy. Isn't it interesting that slang for courageous is "ballsy," and taking a risk is "putting your balls on the line." That's penis talk! Penis doesn't talk about putting itself on the line—that's suicide! *Au contraire*, penis sacrifices his brothers! But the really ballsy male dimension is soft and tender; it is creative and life affirming. Your testicles provide the nonviolent, peace-seeking, peace-making counterbalance to the heat-seeking missile.

But if you are all "nuts," you are weak and passive. It takes a fully developed and balanced man to be powerful and gentle at the same time, and to bring all of himself into his marriage.

As a man, you need to express and use your power outside the home, or you will feel thwarted and may abuse that power at home. This is extremely dangerous. We know of a man who is by nature a powerful warrior but, being married to a successful career woman, is a stay-at-home dad and general fix-it guy. As a result of his not having an outlet for his aggressive power, he is a rage-aholic and tyrant in the house, and at times has his wife cowering in fear. Remember that your power is most frequently very scary to most women.

While we are at it, let's dispel a few other myths. **Men cry.** If you have ever fully grieved over a devastating loss, you know the truth of this. Robert Bly says the core of all men's work is grief work—the digging into the dirt and grieving over all the wounds of battle and for our fallen comrades. Make no mistake about it—when men cry it is deep and heartfelt. **Men feel**—just as deeply and passionately as they grieve. We have a close buddy who always says, "Sure I feel—I feel with my hands!" But we know him to be one of the most deeply passionate and religious men around, and when our mutual teammate lost a child, he wept as only a man and devoted father can. Foremost of all, *men commit*. The propaganda that men do not commit is a plot to discredit our gender and bring us into submission!

(OK—that is a little strong, but frankly, the whole idea pisses us off). Men commit to what is important to them—quickly, deeply, often, and without fear. It is what distinguishes "real" men—their commitment! We know very few women who would go into battle over a principle. Oh, women will fight fiercely, but mostly if you threaten their children or family. They are too smart and sophisticated to kill each other over concepts. Men will. And men do that because of their commitments.

One last thing: at the martial arts dojo, we wear a cup to protect ourselves from a misdirected front kick. However, we do not suggest that you wear some relationship cup to protect your softness in your relationship! You will certainly have disagreements in your marriage. If you are all dick, then you'll go to battle with your wife, and if you're all nuts you'll let her have her way. But if you're balanced, you'll work it out so that both of you win. And one last reminder: if you haven't noticed, your wife has both hard and soft sides too. She's not above kicking you squarely in the nuts.

> *Survival Tip:* Be aware of where you are too much dick (toughness) and not enough balls (vulnerability) or too soft and not enough of the rock. Both your wife and the relationship need your full masculinity.

It's Not about You (Really)

I f you want to have a powerful, flowing, loving relationship with your woman, then you had best realize that the relationship is not about you. Life is rarely about you, so why should marriage be any different.

Sometimes it is so hard to be in relationship. It seems like a constant competition for position—especially if and when you throw in a couple of kids. Who is right? Who is wrong? What is really going on? Where do I fit in? Do I even matter? These are all important questions *if you really don't care about your woman*. But if you do, what really matters is that you not make it about you, and just love her. As Don Henley says in the song by the same name, "Get over it!"

Sound easy? WRONG! It is probably the hardest thing you will ever do in your life. It may be the only thing you never fully learn. That is why we said earlier that you must take this on as a discipline. A good woman will send tests your way in modified forms to see if you will budge or compromise on your commitment to love her. The moment you make it about you, you have failed the test.

Engaging in any debate will make it about you; for example, let's say that she says that you don't look at her the way you used to when you first met. There are maybe four or five ways you could handle this.

You may know in your heart that you *do* look at her the way you used to, and you try to convince her that you're right and she's wrong by turning the tables: you say that *she* just doesn't *notice* how lovingly you look at her. You explain that you're doing it right now, but she is so wrapped up in whatever that she can't see how much you love her. Then you move to a more offensive mode. You ask her why she thinks you don't do that anymore, or you actually try to explain why. Or maybe you *haven't* been looking at her the way you used to, and you make excuses: you're tied up at work, or have lots on your mind, or some other thing that makes her feel like a low priority. Or you could always blame her: maybe if she were nicer to you, you would be more attentive. Oh, and the last one: you play dumb—you have no idea what she's talking about, and why is she bringing this up now? I think you get the idea.

This is the danger zone! We would say stop, but what we want you to do is DON'T START!

Allow us to propose a different option. Don't make it about you. Let her have her moment. Even if you think she is in the wrong and you are innocent of the charges, don't take it personally. You just need to let whatever happens unfold, and love her through it all.

There is no immediate resolution to a conflict like this. But when you make it about you, you have extended the completion time, and you have the power to extend it indefinitely. We think this is one of the reasons for divorce. Too many men just have to be right and take the disagreement personally! We have heard men say that their wives were making their lives miserable, when in reality they were making themselves miserable by insisting on being right in the face of a woman who doesn't really care about right or wrong in that moment (even if it looks like she is trying to make you wrong). She is just trying to tell you something, and that something is not about you. It is about her. Whatever you did or did not do may have triggered it (or not), but that doesn't make it about you. Here is the trick: she may be saying, "When you did this or that, you made me feel thus or so..." but even then, it is not about you! She is just telling you how SHE feels. Let her say and do what she needs to in order to get through it. Even if she doesn't get through it, she will eventually burn out, run out of gas, and (ya gotta love this) give up.

You can either be right or you can be happy—you can't be both. Look: if you were in a high school debate society, it would be important to be right. But it doesn't matter in your marriage. Let us say that again: being right does NOT matter. What matters is that you love your wife, which requires that you not judge her and not make her wrong. Your need to be right comes from what Wayne Levine calls the "Little Boy" who always wants Mommy's approval.[17] Grow up.

Another mistake that is easy to make is trying to understand what's going on in her mind. Why is she behaving so irrationally? You will never really know what she wants, even if she has stated it repeatedly. You must be the sponge wall for her to throw her stuff against. Your job is to absorb it, not make it about you, and love her through it all. Your woman is emotional; accept it and get over it—she just is (see "Women and Emotions" in the next section).

> *Survival Tip:* Practice silencing the little boy who wants his mommy's attention. Being an adult male means learning that your life is not yours.

---

17 Levine, *N.U.T.s*, p. 57.

AND BABY MAKES THREE

"The most important thing a father can do for his
children is to love their mother."

Theodore Hesburgh

One of the more significant changes in a marriage is the arrival of your little bundle of joy. For many men this signals the end of being the center of their wives' attention—as well it should be. Babies require not only a lot of attention, they are dependent on their moms for warmth and sustenance. But more importantly, a mother's experience seems best summed up in a saying I heard once and is stitched on a pillow my wife has: "The decision to have a child is to accept that forever your heart will walk around outside of your body" (K. Hadley).

Literally, then, the gestation and delivery of another life alters the entity formerly known as your wife. And while many men prepare in much the same way (scientists have now found that men undergo hormonal changes triggered by their wives' hormonal shifts), it still is not the same, and bonding at birth and in early infancy only partially replicates what your wife has experienced and provided over the past nine months. But remember this guide is not about her.

The shifting of focus that many men experience is their fall from stardom. And the degree to which you are upset by that is the degree to which you had ascribed your self-worth to your wife. This is extremely important to get—because that which you give away is not yours to bring to the marriage relationship. If you needed your wife to "make you whole" then you were not whole; as a result, you were not giving her a complete and fully functioning husband. "Needing" your wife for your self-definition will be discussed in the next section, but for now, as Levine says, you need to silence that whining "little boy"—quickly and for good![18]

Of course, we all have "needs." But to burden your wife, or more accurately, your relationship, with the task of providing for your needs is unfair and damaging. Recognizing your neediness and meeting those needs through your own resourcefulness, through direction your men's circle can provide, and through your spiritual connection with some source greater than you, is healthy and strengthening for the relationship.

The arrival of a baby is a miracle. But if you find yourself sulking in the corner thinking, "What about me?" then you would be well served by looking inside and inspecting your neediness as a destructive burden on your marriage. Take that to your men and dump it so you can come back home like the man, the father, and the husband we know you can be.

Now let's turn to the shifting role that you have once you become a parent. First of all, we defer to the experts in this field, in this case a superbly well-written book by Dr. Kyle Pruett and

18 Levine, *ibid.*

his spouse called *Partnership Parenting*.[19] What the Pruetts have done is place the role of the father alongside the mass of literature on women and mothering which has dominated the field of parenting literature. Furthermore, it is clear that Dr. Pruett understands masculinity as we describe it and has given voice to the importance of bringing a fully functional masculinity into the role of fathering.

As fathers, we are not "replacement mothers" as the Pruetts point out. We have a triple role to play: father, teammate on the family cluster called the child's team, and supporter of mother as she performs her functions, duties, and roles. As is our contention regarding marriage success, the critical element in Partnership Parenting is the process of resolving the differences. Literally, the problems of differences are the source of the strength the family unit can define. And nothing will push you further than the birth and addition of (even if through adoption) a new member of your family.

So just what is the role of the father? The masculine energy as well as the playfulness and creativity we bring as fathers is essential for our offspring. Our job as fathers is not only to model healthy "balanced" masculinity, but to take an active role in caring for and parenting our children. Women whose husbands take an active role in child care and child raising report feeling like they are being directly cared for themselves.[20] If you are new to parenting, pick up a copy of the Pruett's book.

> *Survival Tip:* Don't expect your wife to be your mother and don't demand that the relationship provide you with what your men should.

---

19 Kyle Pruett, MD, and Marsha Kline Pruett, PhD, *Partnership Parenting: How Men and Women Parent Differently—Why It Helps Your Kids and Can Strengthen Your Marriage*, Da Capo Press, Cambridge, MA, 2009.

20 Pruett, p. 29.

Not Needing Your Woman

Now here is an additional piece of the puzzle that would be helpful to nail in order to increase your survival chances. You need to get to a level of self-worth where you do not need your woman—at all, for anything. We regularly say this to men before they get married, and we firmly believe that we save marriages in advance. What we mean is, if you approach your marriage from a perspective of needing something from her for your self-esteem, for your well-being, or for your ego's sake, you are using her. Your marriage is not about you. It is about her. And when you are needy, you make it all about you. And what's more, you become whiney. A good test of whether or not you need her is how much you whine and bitch and moan (even to your buddies). Neediness, whining, bitching, and moaning are the sure signs of an overactive and out-of-control little boy.

Here is the key: when you do not NEED her, you are then able to approach her as a free choice. You can actually CHOOSE her— and in doing so, you validate HER. It is as if you could have any woman in the entire world, and *you choose her!* It is the most powerful thing you can do to enhance your relationship, and you must keep choosing her, over and over again.

This plays out in the nitty-gritty of sex. You may want sex—it's programmed and brainwashed into you. But do you NEED sex? You do? What for—to get your rocks off? Fine; then masturbate. *You don't need sex.* The uninitiated adolescent in your head wants a release of his pent-up hormones, or needs some bragging rights, but YOU do not need sex. The species will survive without you! We will go so far as to assert that if you need her for sex, you are doing nothing more than masturbating using a vagina instead of your hand.

But when you come to her out of choosing HER—all of her —you can pleasure her and adore her and "make love" to her in the purest and most fulfilling way she has ever experienced. See, it really is not about you—ever!

> *Survival Tip:* Practice catching yourself when you are needy with your wife. Then determine whether you really need whatever it is, and if so, find somewhere else to get it (preferably from or with your men.)

BEING THE BEST YOU CAN BE

Now that you have an idea of what it takes to be a self-sufficient, powerful, balanced, ego-less man, we have two questions. What is your personal best? How do you know what the best you can do is? In marriage, you need to become whole and to get into the discipline of giving your absolute best at every moment. You cannot let up because the moment you do will be the one time that she will need to rely on you. From the very beginning of this guide we have talked about disciplines, and dedicated one of the first chapters to it (and just to warn you, we will end the entire guide that way as well). We now want to focus that and shift away from the relationship back to the core of your being. Your personal discipline must be what shapes and forms you into your very best.

Before you can be truly disciplined, you must establish what you stand for and what you are committed to; otherwise, what's the point? Many men are incredibly disciplined in their work, their physical fitness or other aspects of their lives. But if there is no context or framework for the discipline, it can be just an empty habit, and the success it brings is hollow. Likewise, if you have no context, framework, or driving value in your marriage it is rendered meaningless as well.

These values are called your terms or your unalterable stand. Terms are conditions you impose on yourself, and they define you and your integrity. They have nothing to do with anyone else; for example, you may take a stand that "dinner is a family event in my house." But that involves others, so that stand is a desire or a command, but it is not a core term. Your terms apply to yourself, and no one else.[21] "I will never compromise my values of honesty and trust," is a term—a statement of what you expect of yourself— and either you uphold that or you are out of integrity with yourself.

Mahatma Gandhi taught what he called the "single decision."[22] What he said was that you should strive to make a decision clearly and then never have to think of that again. Make your terms such "single decisions." Once you have discovered your purpose in life and defined your terms, you should never have to revisit those decisions again.

Once you get clear on what you stand for in life, your commitments become very clear. Your commitments flow from your purpose, your terms and whatever it is that you are doing. In this way, everything you do—your job, your hobbies, even your vacations—becomes a unified expression of who you are. And when this happens, you become solid and consistent for everyone around you—especially for your wife. Your consistency and focus become anchors for her and for the family, and this makes a huge difference in the quality of the relationship. Work with your men's team to get clear on your unalterable stand and your terms.

---

21 Levine, *N.U.T.s*, p. 35.

22 Keshavan Nair, *A Higher Standard of Leadership, Lessons from the life of Gandhi*, Berrett-Koehler Publishers, San Francisco, CA, 1994, p. 31.

Adopt the practice of living by your commitments. This requires that you start each day by making a single commitment that you will fulfill that day. Now, do yourself a favor and don't just pick something like committing to brushing your teeth three times that day! Nice hygiene but no traction! Make a commitment that matters, something that will stretch you as a man, and make sure it is consistent with your purpose and your terms.

However, there is a little matter with which you will inevitably have to contend. The universe runs according to a set of very powerful and unyielding laws, and one of these affects your fulfillment of your commitments. That law is Newton's third law: "for every action there is an equal and opposite reaction." Your commitment is one such *action* and the universe will welcome it with an equal and opposite reaction—that means the more powerful your commitment, the more powerfully negative the reaction will be. In fact, you should look for the equal and opposite reaction as an indicator of the nature of your commitment. If there is no reaction, you probably have not committed to anything of worth. But if something comes up immediately and smacks you in the face, pat yourself on the back and know that you are making one helluva big commitment—that's when you get to work!

Still confused? Wayne Levine does a really good job discussing terms in his book, *Hold On To Your N.U.T.S.*[23]

But we need to move on.

> *Survival Tip:* If you want to see your terms in living color, take a good, long look at how you are living your life right now. Write down everything you do, both habits and commitments—these are your terms.

---

23 Levine, *N.U.T.s*, p. 35.

SECTION 3

PROVIDING SHELTER

"Good men and good women have fire in the belly. We are fierce.
Don't mess with us if you are looking for somebody who will always be
'nice' to you. ('Nice' gets you a C+ in life.) We don't always smile, talk
in a soft voice, or engage in indiscriminate hugs. In the loving struggle
between the sexes we thrust and parry."

Sam Keen

Getting caught above tree line with an approaching storm is a vulnerable and life-threatening situation—you need to seek shelter, fast! Knowing how to read the skies and signs can prevent disaster. In marriage, this translates to reading your woman's signs: moods, emotions, and language. This section outlines what to do and how to read those signs of impending storms.

(Kris and Dave)

WOMEN AND EMOTIONS

"Women are not liars. The feminine says what it feels. A woman's
word is her true expression in the moment."
David Deida

Y ou may have noticed that your woman is a tad more emotional than you. In general, women are more adept at this
essential human function than men are. This is actually
by design and can be the source of quite a number of issues, dis-
turbances, and misunderstandings. Earlier, in the Introduction for
Women, we referred to Rob Becker's *Defending the Caveman*. He says
that it all boils down to the fact that men evolved as hunters and
women as gatherers. In order to be good hunters, early men had to
be quiet, stay focused on their visual field and the sounds of the
savannah, and suppress their fear. They communicated nonverbally
with simple hand and body signals that transmitted only vital information. In contrast, early women evolved with more developed
taste, smell, and touch—the more emotional senses—in order to

be able to test the fruits for ripeness. And they had to react to their senses with emotion—yummy (happy), yucky (disgusted)—to make decisions about the fruit. Early women also had to communicate these emotions to each other in order to gather successfully, so they evolved the ability to effectively express a wide array of emotions.

It's been a relatively short amount of time in evolutionary terms since then, so today, you basically have "cavemen" and "cavewomen" running around in business suits, sitting in three-hour meetings about sales projections, and evaluating data and making decisions using different skills. Then they go home to their spouses, where they have to maintain their "relationship" with those same dissimilar skills. The problems generated by the emotional gap between men and women stem not from women's emotions but rather from men's lack of understanding of them. So, to prevent this gap from driving you and your wife crazy and destroying your marital bliss, get the following through your testosterone-stoked head:

<u>Emotions are not logical.</u> This statement makes perfect sense, but we men don't really accept it as true. We want to know "why" she feels that way. The answer (if you are actually stupid enough to pursue that course of inquiry) is "because, that's how I feel!" Feelings do not need a reason; to a "gatherer," feelings are the source themselves. "These berries feel ripe" is no different in her world than "I don't feel like cleaning the house," or "I feel like you don't appreciate me." These statements need no explanation, evidence, or logical support. They are complete thoughts and are, from a woman's point of view, self-evident. Of course there is a cause, but knowing that will make no difference to either you or her. Stop asking, or even wondering "Why?" and "What makes you feel that way?" Emotions are emotional, not logical.

<u>Emotions do not need fixing.</u> They just are—they exist and must be reported on by your woman. So put away your tool kit; there is nothing wrong that must be righted when she says she feels sad or mad or confused or scared. What she is doing is telling you how she feels, *just so you know.* We men, on the other hand want to right the wrong immediately. If we screwed up, we want to fix it, and if she did wrong, we want to "help" her. Don't. The best answer to a report on feelings is a simple, "Oh," followed by—if you can muster the wherewithal to remember this—"tell me about it." We men think of emotions as directional indicators: feel fear—run away; feel attraction—go toward; feel confused—get more data. We are simple like that. But they—our delightfully beautiful and complex partners—are far more subtle. An emotional report-out is often a hint to explore and listen more, but not to dialogue (see the section on "Listening," later in this chapter). That is important to remember—shut up and listen.

Her emotions are not *yours.* This is big. PAY ATTENTION! Even when she says, "You make me feel…" it is not about you (if you haven't gotten that yet, go back and reread the "It's Not About You," section). Rather, she is telling you how she feels, and that is all. Just because she is upset, it does not mean (or require) that you must also be upset. Because she is crying, it does not mean that you have to be tearful as well. She is feeling stuff—let her feel it. Thank God at least one of you has the capacity for feeling! The real cool thing for you to do here is tap into her vast vocabulary and talent for identifying feelings. She can be the best sensor you could ever find—better than a Star Trek© Tricorder ("No visible life forms here, Captain."). Ask her to name her feelings (she'll love that!).

<u>This works both ways.</u> Here is another thing to note about feelings: you can tell her how you feel about commitments, work,

life, and things in general without ever having to explain. When she asks why you feel that way, all you need ever say is, "I don't know, it's just how I feel." She will accept that as a legitimate answer but remember, you need only tell her the feeling and not explain or defend it. That will only get you in trouble because her knowledge of that territory is so much greater and more sophisticated than yours. Your actual rationale will not hold water under scrutiny. Just tell her how you feel about whatever is up at the time.

Don't get us wrong here: we are not contending that men do not have feelings or that men cannot express those feelings (especially those among us who are trained at ISNAG, the Institute of Sensitive New-Age Guys). We certainly are, as humans, fully capable of the complete range and depth of human emotions. In fact, I would venture that our understanding of grief and pain is greater in some cases than any woman's is. We have listened to the stories of veterans who are grieving their fallen brothers, and the depth of the pain they feel, and we know that particular feeling is most unique to Warriors. Any man who has ever been in a lights-out grieving session for men knows how deep that vein is. We are simply contending that we are not nearly as accomplished and versatile at expressing and articulating feelings in general. Around your men, you can learn how to talk about your feelings. You need a safe place in which to practice that but because it puts you in a vulnerable and undefended place, it is not wise to practice that with her!

Survival Tip: Stop looking for logical explanations to why she feels the way she does. Emotions are not logical and she is just reporting her state to you. Practice being thankful when your wife tells you how she feels. See if this helps you to stop wondering why or trying to fix.

HER EMOTIONAL STATE SETS THE TONE

"A woman's sense of self is defined through her feelings
and the quality of her relationships."
John Gray

I t has been said that "when Mama ain't happy, ain't nobody happy," and perhaps nothing could be more true. Your woman's emotional state determines the level of communication and re-latedness you enjoy at any given time. When she is down, it will seem to suck the life out of the relationship, and no amount of fixing it on your part will make it better. She will always set the emotional tone of the relationship.

Anyway, when she feels something, she will persist in that feeling until she is done; and you cannot "fix" that. Because her emotional state is a roller coaster by its very nature, your relation-ship will have its ups and downs. As much as you would like the state of your marriage to be more like a boat ride on the lake, it is not and will never be. Emotions simply do not have that quality— e-motions are always *in* motion. Therefore, your life together will be filled with surprises around every corner. Learn to monitor your woman's emotional state. It will serve you well to know her cycles and moods—if for nothing else, to remind you that her emotions don't dictate yours.

One great way to try to understand her cycles and moods is this. Pretend that you are a fly on the wall of a conversation your woman is having with her girlfriend. She is talking about you. What is she saying? Depending on her emotional state, she would say anything from "He is the best man," to "That mother f@#s no-good life-sucking bastard." You can probably narrow this down to five or six references. It is important to pay attention to what emotional state your woman may be in, because everything you do will have a reaction from that emotional state.

Let's say you were asked to bring home milk and you forgot. We would presume that if your woman's emotional state is "He is the greatest guy in the world," then forgetting to bring home milk would really have little to no repercussions. But if you forgot to bring home milk and your woman was thinking, "That mother f@#s no-good life-sucking bastard," we would presume that not bringing home milk would be a huge deal.

And just for shits and giggles, we are going to say one more thing about women's emotions. Did you ever notice that your woman can be in the most torrid knock-down, drag-out screaming contest with you, and when the phone rings, she is able to answer in a sweet and pleasant voice, "Oh, hi, Amy...oh nothing...sure (fill in the rest)." And the really astounding part is that, upon hanging up, she is still pissed and can go right back at it! We have no explanation for this and are just as baffled as you are. If the same thing happens when the phone is near you, you would probably either ignore it and stay in the fight or pick it up and bark something obnoxious into the receiver before slamming it back down. This is one of those times when you have to just accept that she can do that, and hold your place in the "conversation" to be resumed when she hangs up, or better yet, use the time to shift your consciousness and let go of your need to be right. When she comes back to the discussion, you can be ready to just listen.

Another important principle of human relationships is that none of us can accept any amount of love greater than that which we feel for ourselves. While you may not notice this limit in yourself, it is very important be aware of it in your wife. If you try to give her more love than she believes she deserves, she will simply not let it in. The reverse is also true. Your wife can't love you more than you love yourself. And if she can't love you as much as she wants to, the relationship doesn't have much of a chance. Moreover, as Alison Armstrong says, a woman won't let you love her more than she loves herself, if you try to, she will devalue it until you are at or below her level. Now would be time for a great story about one of us. (David) I don't remember why, but I had done something bad. Really bad. My wife was in "That mother f@#s no-good life-sucking bastard" mode. I think I did not make the bed that morning. Anyway, I decided that I would bring home flowers, tell her that I love her very much, and apologize. I picked up a dozen tulips (her favorite), and brought them home. I gave her the tulips, and told her sincerely that I was sorry. She immediately took the tulips, and made a three point shot to the wastebasket. I got it. Tulips were the wrong choice. I loved her more than tulips. I got back into my car, went back to the flower shop, and bought a dozen red roses, baby's breath, wrapping and all. This was an expression of my love for my wife. I brought them home, gave them to my wife, told her that I was sorry and that I loved her very much. Again, another three pointer! Score, 6-0. Like a puppy with his tail between his legs, I went back to the flower store and bought all the red roses they had (twenty-six of them). I came back home and gave them to my wife. I told her that she was worth every red rose they had in the flower shop. I told her that I loved her more than anything else in the world, and I was sorry. Score? You guessed it! 9-0.

In this case, I loved my wife more than she loved me and it did not work. Our relationship was limited by how much love she was willing to give and accept. I could have easily come home and told her I was sorry, saved myself two hundred dollars, and achieved the same result.

This story could unfold differently for different men. Remember, each woman is different and reacts differently to situations. Her emotional state sets the tone.

As Alison Armstrong coaches her female readers, a woman's lack of self esteem and inability to receive are the two biggest factors that suck the juice out of any relationship. But the other two, a lack of passion and authenticity, seal it shut.[24] Among the things that negatively impact passion and authenticity are her weight, her period, her job, the drain and strain of the kids, and sometimes even the news of a puppy falling down a well. Obviously, just as there is nothing you can do about her emotional state, you are even more powerless against the state of her self-esteem, her passion, or her authenticity; just be aware, accept that it's not about you, and keep on loving her.

Survival Tip: Notice how your wife's moods and emotional states affect you. Find ways to stay on top of your game all the time, especially when her emotions are down.

---

24 Armstrong, *Making Sense*, p. 59.

LISTENING

"Relationships are made of talk—and talk is for girls and women."

Deborah Tannen

Women do not speak English. They come from a region of the Galaxy called Hint and speak what may sound like English, but is really the highly sophisticated Zen-like language of Hintish.[25] Hintish is a way of saying things without saying them, a way of alluding indirectly to some feeling or request. It's crucial that you learn to recognize when your wife is speaking Hintish, and to decode it so that you cannot only save countless hours trying to get to the point of a conversation, but also impress her with your marital skill. Perhaps someday, someone will write a Hintish to (male) English dictionary, but in the meantime, we will give you the flavor of this exotic and mysterious tongue.

---

[25] We would like to credit our friend Kent Johnson with coming up with the term "Hintish." It's one of those truths that you hear in your circle that just sticks! Thanks, Kent!

When she says something like, "What a beautiful, sunny day!" she may really mean, "Will you help me plant all the flowers I spent $250 on, and then dig them up again so that I can have you replant them to see if they look better this way or that?" Or, depending on the intonation, it could mean, "Let's go for a nice walk along the beach."

When she says, "I really wish you didn't have to stay late at work," it might mean, "I want to get a babysitter so we can go out and have some much needed together time." Or, "I'm horny."

You get the idea. The secret to translating her speech is LISTEN-ING. Listening is an art form that you must master by disciplined practice. But it's like jazz: the music (her Hintish) is always evolving, changing, never the same twice, and you as the listener must stay alert and connected so you can improvise and stay in the flow.

The big mistake men make in listening is they open their mouths. The moment you open your trap, you are doing just that, setting a trap. Guess who gets sprung in the trap: you do! Saying just about anything will create an environment where she will think you are *not* listening and she will have to start over from square one. If you want to know what she is really saying, you have to wait and wait, listen and listen, stare into her eyes, and love her through her mass of emotions until she gets it all out. Then you have a shot at having some kind of conversation. But the bottom line is you have only ONE duty as the male partner in the relationship. Just one: LISTEN!

Now there is listening and there is LISTENING! The latter is an advanced version that listens beyond the words (the content—the "what") of her message, to the background values and commitments (the intent—the "why") that drive the communication. If you want to become a master of listening, you need to learn how to listen for both the "why" and the "what" of the conversation.

At one point, Kris and his wife were in a particularly busy time and both of them were going 120 mph. One evening they actually had supper together, and when Kris got up from the table, he took his plate and silverware and put them in the sink. In a rather irritated voice, his lovely partner said, "Why do you put your dishes in the sink when the dishwasher is open right beside the sink and clearly has dirty dishes in it?" Now, the response to the *content* would be, "Oh, right!" and place the dishes in the dishwasher. But listening to the *intent* behind it, he said instead, "Hey, thanks for being committed to efficiency when we're both on a zoom like we are." Her only response was, "Um, yeah, that's what I meant!"

Think of it this way. If a work colleague comes to you for help making a presentation for the annual sales meeting, he might have several reasons: 1) you are the expert in this area, so he is deferring to you; 2) it's a politically charged situation and he doesn't like ruffling feathers; 3) he never learned PowerPoint; Wouldn't you respond differently to each? But your wife won't tell you her intent directly, so you will have to figure out the intent of what she is saying, and respond to that.

One day, Dave's wife had a presentation to make at work. She was worried about how she would do, and if her colleagues would get behind her ideas. When she came home that evening, it did not take long for her to let him know the house was a mess, the kid's homework was not done, and dogs needed to be fed. It took him a moment to muster what he wanted to say about all this, because, in fact, he had picked up the house, fed the dogs, and homework was handled. Instead of reacting to what she said, Dave sent the children upstairs, turned off the TV, poured her a glass of wine, and asked her how her presentation went. She then talked about how her colleagues did not get behind what she believed in, how they were not receptive to her ideas, and how she felt unappreciated for her hard work and ideals.

Once you have learned how to identify the intent behind what your wife is saying, you need to respond appropriately to it, which is difficult and not a little tricky. It's tricky because not only does she speak a different language, but your wife doesn't even know that you don't speak or understand it too. As a result, she may assume that: 1) you will answer the embedded question directly, and/or; 2) your answer will be in Hintish as well—ergo, she will intuit all manner of implications from whatever you say. Alison Armstrong makes an interesting observation that explains why this is: Most women think of men as "hairy, more muscular, uncouth women."[26]

So in order to get past these assumptions, you must learn how to tell her that you understand her intent, and that you want to listen some more. Try using language like: "I think I understand that what you are saying is (then say it), but it sounds like (the intent that you think is behind it) is what's up for you. Can we talk about that?" If you are wrong she'll no doubt tell you (she will definitely notice and appreciate the effort), but if you are right—and this is important— you need to ask permission to talk about it; otherwise, you put her on the defensive and she will feel very exposed and vulnerable. This may sound awkward, and it may not be how you are used to relating to your wife, but believe us, it works. To get good at it, you can (and should) practice these communication skills with your men.

Remember that, even though you asked, "Can we *talk* about that?" what you really do next is—you guessed it—listen. And then it starts all over again; you listen for the intent, echo that back to her, and ask if it's OK talk about it some more (which is Hintish for "I'll listen"). And so on, until she's done. When you have mastered these skills and can go for several rounds like this with your wife, you will know that you are a world-class listener (and husband).

---

26 Armstrong, p.11. Actually, she dedicates an entire chapter to the subject of how women expect us to think like them (and, by the way, she rightly points out that men assume women are just softer, better-smelling men).

Extreme Listening

The other aspect of Hintish that you must pay attention to is the emotion behind the words. That is often the real subject of the conversation. But if her emotion is especially intense or deep, your wife may have to talk a lot to get to the point of letting you know what her emotion is, and she won't get there until she feels vulnerable and trusting enough to reveal that. If you get into this situation, we have a few suggestions.

The first tip is to listen some more. Usually men give up way too soon because it gets too hard. When your woman is calling you names and telling you how useless you are, you must realize that this is bait to get you engaged. Saying those things is her way to see if she can trust you enough for her to go to that vulnerable place. If you take the bait and react or blow up, you will stop listening, and she will know that she can't trust you and close down. If you fail to create that safe place for her to open up (and especially if you blow up and get in a screaming fight), she will see you as untrustworthy, and the next time she needs to let you know how she feels, it will be twice as hard. If you fail enough times, you may lose her; at best, you will have set the stage for a dead marriage.

But if you hang in there and don't give up, the second thing you should do is—you got it—listen some more. You could think of it as a great exercise in discipline, to not quit on the process. The point where you feel like you can't stand it anymore is probably when you are closest to being successful and becoming a hero in her eyes! Hang in there a little longer.

Have you ever been arguing with your wife and she called you a name. Take some time and think about it. "You _____!" Fill in the blank. If you take the words literally, it is easy to make up the definition.

Here are some definitions, I am sure you can figure out the words.

> The hole where my crap comes out of in the morning
> A man whose sexual preference is with other men
> A man who sucks the members of other men
> A person who loses especially consistently
> A person whose head looks like shit
> A person whose head resembles a penis

Think back to the last time you thought you were listening to your woman. Take a minute to run that movie through your brain again from start to finish. Got it? Great! Now remember what she said she wanted or needed or what you did wrong, what you did not do, or even better did not do the way she thought you should do it.

Now think ahead one hour after that conversation, or one day or one week. Do you remember ever having figured out what was really going on? Here is a list of just some of the things your woman most likely wanted you to listen for:

I hurt
I am scared
I don't feel loved or loveable anymore
The kids seem to suck the life out of me
This is a thankless, colorless, stupid role—being a
mom/wife/housekeeper
I am tired
(well you get the picture)

Did you ever notice hearing any of those statements coming out of her mouth? No, we didn't think so. You heard, "You ass, I hate you!" The distinction we want you to get here is that when your men call you a dickhead, you are a dickhead. But when your wife calls you a dickhead, she means one of the above. Your job is to listen for that.

If you still think she is not willing to get where she needs to go, then leave. Don't storm out of the house, and never use the exact words "I'M LEAVING!" If you want to create a feeling of abandonment with your woman, say those words. Instead, tell her you have to do something that you forgot to do, turn off some thing down in the garage, get milk at the store, buy some socks, or anything you can think of. Be sincere. Let her know you can continue the conversation when you return. Tell her you love her, and then find a way to get out of her presence.

Usually what happens when you leave is that it gives her time to do whatever she does to move forward with that emotion. It may also give her time to create a new plan of attack. She must go through this process alone, or with one of her women friends, without you. It's OK—remember, you don't have to fix her. So go ahead, go buy those socks!

Survival Tip: Practice listening with your men. Have one of them play the part of your wife, calling you every name in the book and pointing out everything that's wrong with you. Have the other men voice encouragement to you to hang in there and keep listening. See if you can hear them next time your wife starts in on you.

YOUR TIME OUT

Take your time; fifteen to forty-five minutes should suffice. Longer makes her think you "ran away," and shorter may not be enough time for you and her to regroup. How does she regroup? We don't really need or want to know, and neither should you. But how you regroup is important to discuss, because she will need all of you when you return, and she will need you to be able to listen. Forgive yourself and her for what is going on. There may be no right or wrong in the situation at hand. Allowing her to feel listened to, should she accept, is an incredible gift you can give to her. You will have to take baby steps to master this. You will not get it right the first time. Don't think about the words. Don't think about the situation. Forget about it. Forget the details, the words, the threats, the accusations, and everything else except for one thing: that your job is to listen and create that safe space for her to be vulnerable and open up. (So if you need more detail on how to forgive and forget, we will cover that later at the end of section 5.) Not thinking about it, getting over it and coming back fresh allows you to take a fresh approach and a new look at being the quality of a man that will allow her to be vulnerable and loving.

And you are the one who wins when she is vulnerable and loving.

A woman seeks a man who will listen and allow her to be vulnerable in her darkest moments. Being that man is easy work when you let go of what you think the journey is supposed to look like and remember what your job really is.

There is a great poem by e.e. cummings[27] that says it well.

all which isn't singing is mere talking
and all talking's talking to oneself
(whether that oneself be sought or seeking
master or disciple sheep or wolf)

gush to it as deity or devil
—toss in sobs and reasons threats and smiles
name it cruel fair or blessed evil—
it is you (ne i)nobody else

drive dumb mankind dizzy with haranguing
—you are deafened every mother's son-
all is merely talk which isn't singing
and all talking's to oneself alone

but the very song of(as mountains
feel and lovers)singing is silence

(Hey, no one ever said we couldn't be cultured!) We think Cummings understood this point. When *you* feel the need to talk when your woman is trying to convey *her* feelings, that qualifies as talking to yourself. Shut your yap! This is all about her needing to convey something.

---

27 Courtesy of Poem Hunter: http://www.poemhunter.com/poem/all-which-isn-t-singing-is-mere-talking/

Men convey way better than women. We are blunt and to the point. Your wife is not a man, which is, by the way, why you love her. Be her lover and be silent.

Survival Tip: The greatest skill you can practice in a relationship is silent, attentive listening. Shut up and pay attention!

THEORY OF THE FEMALE UNIVERSE

One day, after hearing (not listening) to his wife tell him that he always makes her wrong about everything, Dave made a brilliant well-thought-out response. He believed it was his greatest work. It was the thing that was going to solve all their relationship problems. Man, was it good. Dave's game-changing, magnificently brilliant response was

"No I don't!"

There is a term for this kind of response: "coming from No." No, she was wrong. No, she didn't understand me. No, she didn't know what she was talking about. No, the relationship was not in as bad a shape as she was describing. No, No, No.

Pay attention to when you are in No. No is a very powerful emotional word to a woman. When you bring No to the surface, you create a hostile environment, which is as destructive to the relationship as blowing up and getting into a screaming fight. When you come from No, you are discounting what she is feeling, invalidating her, and making her wrong. The last thing you want to do is make her wrong, even if she is.

When you are in No, YOU start a no-win process for the relationship. Once you start coming from No, she will return with a bigger and better No, and will keep doing that until she has diminished you as a man, or you surrender. She wins, but the relationship loses. Or, she will give up, withdraw, and resent the hell out of you. Again, the relationship loses. But all she really wanted in the first place was to be heard.

It is OK for you to be wrong, even if you are not. When you are playing sports, there are rules. It is easy to decide who is right or wrong based on the rules. If the runner gets tagged with the ball while he is running, he is out. That is the rule. If the soccer ball goes in the opponent's net, it is one point for the team. That is the rule. With your woman, the rule is "What she believes to be right in this moment is what it shall be." It should not

> One interviewee with 53 years of monogamous marriage gave this advice: "Decide what is really important and let everything else go.

be important for you to be right. What is important is that she gets to say what she needs to say and be right about it. As long as you do not violate your ethics (that is, she is not asking you to commit murder for her), who cares about right and wrong? The relationship is more important than your being right—it is more important than your adamant "NO."

We asked a friend of ours, a man with fifty-nine years of successful marriage, what his secret was, and he put it simply as, "You have to decide what is important and then just let go of all the rest!"

Are you man enough to stand in front of your best buddy and take what he has to give you? Are you man enough to defend against an attack or place your body in harm's way to protect an innocent person, or a child? Whether you are a nonviolent resister or a valiant fighter, you are a man. And a man will stand his ground. So that being the case, you need to be man enough to stand there and defend your relationship against your own ego and take what your wife is dishing out—without having to resort to No.

You should almost never come from No in a relationship. We say almost, because there are some battles that you have to fight, and those are the most important ones, and will be the same ones you will have to defend until you die.

WHEN TO SAY NO

Your core values define who you are as a man.

You have acquired these traits as you matured, and these are the unmovable qualities about you as a man.

Trying to change these traits is impossible and any attempt to do so will diminish who you are. Wayne Levine calls these core principles your N.U.T.s—your Nonnegotiable, Unalterable Terms.[28] Changing or compromising them would be as painful as cutting off your nuts!

Who are you as a man? Think about it. What are the things that make you who you are? The good and the bad. You don't have to think too hard. Look at how you are living your life now. It is no different from when you were younger. These things make your stomach churn when you are not doing them, or when they are threatened with change. Make a list. It is important for you to know what that is because you will have to make some decisions later in this chapter that may be disturbing.

---

28 Levine, *N.U.T.s.*

Here are some things I know about me (Dave)

> No matter what I am doing, if work calls I take care of it.
> I provide for my family no matter what.
> I am on time or early for anything I do.
> I won't eat burnt eggs.
> I make a stand for a safe and prosperous home for my family.
> I have to be in charge.
> I get lazy sometimes.
> I can't remember dates like birthdays and such.

His list is not long, and neither should yours be.

Some of those are nonnegotiable terms and some are just strong preferences. You need to know the difference. Again, Wayne Levine does an exemplary job of making this distinction clear in his book.[29] Read it! What is on your list? Write things down and then go through it and ask which ones you would die defending—like someone suddenly grabbing your little daughter with the intention of kidnapping her (Wayne's example)—might show that one of your terms is, "I protect my family." That is the real test. But burnt eggs, hey, I just don't eat them. When one of those core things is threatened, it is time to say no, but you must be certain that you would be willing to die for that principle, because, more likely than not, saying no will threaten the life of the relationship! And it may even signal its death.

---

29 Levine, *N.U.T.s*, pp. 19-46.

RELATIONSHIP EQUITY ACCOUNT (REA)

For most wives, there is a very simple index of relationship health. It is called the Relationship Equity Account (REA). The REA is like any other bank or equity account. Over time, it will increase or decrease in value, depending on how much is deposited and withdrawn. The currency of the REA is points. Everything you do to make her happy is worth one point. If you spend a million dollars on her, it is worth one point. If you kiss her good-bye in the morning, it is worth one point. In her mind it boils down to, "He cares about me," "I feel special," "I am important to him." After you earn your one point, it's over. It is a one-shot deal (exceptions noted in the Survival Tip).

> Nothing my wife asks me to do is a problem. My wife can fend for herself so if she asks me to do something it must be important to her. So I do it. But, I get to choose which way I show up. I can be a Hero or I can be Victim. One gets me laid; the other leaves me afraid.

You need to contribute to your REA often and consistently. Consistency is important, because as you contribute, your woman will make withdrawals. She reserves the right to make withdrawals of whatever amount she wants, whenever she wants. There are many reasons she makes withdrawals, and we will list the most common. Pay attention here because this is important. Some of these may sound weird, but they are all true and are based on our experiences and those of the many married men we have encountered over the years. She will make heavy withdrawals from the account because:

You forgot to do something you said you would do. Have you ever brought home flowers, and forgot to pick up milk? She will make a withdrawal because you forgot the milk. You did not do what you said you would do. You have become untrustworthy, even if just for the moment. Even if you went back out and got the milk, it would make no difference. You have become inconsistent, and she must make a withdrawal.

You irritate her over nothing. If she asks you to take out the trash or some such trivial thing, just do it. Nothing you could be doing in that moment is important enough to piss her off when you might actually earn a point by doing it cheerfully. If you do it begrudgingly, or with an attitude, or she even senses anything but acceptance in your actions, she will make a withdrawal from the REA.

She doesn't feel taken care of. We could write a whole book on this one, but here is the short summary. "Taken care of" means that she feels safe. It means that she knows that whatever happens, you will take care of her. You will provide stability in her life, but not just financially; you will protect her in the face of any danger, and you will be there for her when she needs you.

She doesn't feel like she is number one. The operative word here is *feel*. Your woman does not have to be number one in your life, but it is important to have her feel that way. A man should have higher priorities in his life than his woman (called his purpose—and for a really good discussion on that refer to David Deida's *Way of the Superior Man*).[30] And if he doesn't, he should take a look at what he would like to leave for a legacy after he is dead. Irrespective of that, he still faces the issue of making his wife *feel* like Numero Uno! How do you do this? Not by faking it, but by focusing on the relationship when you are in it and following the "rules" with discipline.

<u>You love her more than she loves you</u>. Emotionally, a woman needs to be in control, and if you try to love her more than she can love you at that moment, she will need to make a withdrawal, and knock you down a peg or two until that situation is reversed. Researchers (like Deborah Tannen[31]) have found that women learn a value called parity—which means everything in their world should be equal. A love relationship—to your woman—must be on an equal footing.

Keep in mind that if you screw up, or if she thinks you screwed up, she can make a withdrawal for *any* amount of points she wishes. Forgetting to bring home milk could cost you anywhere from one to a hundred points. It is clearly up to her and probably based on how she is feeling at the time, but who knows? Don't try to figure it out!

It's important to remember that, even though she is keeping a running tally, you must not. It would be futile anyway, because only

---

30 David Deida, *The Way of the Superior Man, A Spiritual Guide to Mastering the Challenges of Women, Work and Sexual Desire,* Sounds True, Inc., Boulder, CO, 1997, p. 27.

31 Deborah's first major book, *That's Not What I Meant* (Ballantine Books, 1986), was where we first came across her research, but the most apropos to the discussion might be, *You Just Don't Understand, Women and Men in Conversation,* Ballantine Books, New York, NY, 1991.

she knows the account balance. Your job is to give, and keep giving, without expectation, so that you are crystal clear that you are giving your absolute best. This way of being, and only this way, can make you feel successful in your relationship. Remember, it's not about you, and you don't need her for your own sense of well-being.

If you are giving your best, and things are still not right in her eyes, then something else is going on with her. If this is the case, then it is up to her to get through it and there is not much else you can do. The only thing that you can do is keep listening and giving, and do a lot of praying that it doesn't last long. But just because you can't pull her out of her funk, and your deposits don't seem to be making it into the account, that doesn't mean you quit trying to make them.

> I think that one reason my marriage works is that I consider it the only relationship in my family that has to work. If it even dips to what most people would consider an A-minus, I go about doing what I can to make it better.

In our men's groups, we did an exercise where each of us tallied up a bunch of screwups over the past few weeks, and assigned various points from one to five to each, depending on the severity (decided on by the rest of the team). Then we chose a multiplier depending on the overall mood of our wives: one if she was relatively calm, or very "in love" with us and five if she was on the rampage (she can actually change the valuation based on her emotional state—which is much like when the dollar is down, your stock suffers). The total was our negative equity. One of the men was just beaming despite his score of -93 over the last two weeks, and the others asked him why. "I have a saint," he said, "She still loves me despite my -93 points!" Or was it something else? A quick check revealed that this was a man who had a daily discipline of doing dozens of things for his wife and depositing one point at a time, a hundred times a day.

Survival Tip: Look for "self-regenerating points"[32]—a bouquet of roses, though only a point, when given at work nets a point for each person who comments on them. A diamond pendant yields a point each time her friends say how beautiful it is.

---

[32] Many thanks to one of our great heroes and a true mentor, Rich O'Keeffe, for introducing us to the term.

FIFTEEN MINUTES A DAY

How much time should you invest in your relationship? Keeping things simple, we would recommend fifteen minutes a day. If you spend fifteen minutes a day giving your woman undivided attention and your undivided commitment, she will send you off to conquer the world. Don't be stingy! It took a long time for us to realize that giving that focused time unconditionally to our women provided great benefit for both us and our wives. It allowed us to be generous, and it allowed our wives to feel special. The key here is that during this time, you must be certain that there is no other distraction around—no cell phone or "crackberry," no kids, no phone calls, nothing—absolutely nothing but 100 percent, undivided attention to her. By the way, this is not time spent watching your or her favorite TV show with her. In fifteen minutes of undivided attention, you can literally fill her up. And it will beat two hours of interrupted, half-assed attention, hands down!

Now sometimes you need to give more. Fifteen minutes is only a guideline. Don't start out for a two-mile walk with her and turn around and go home halfway through. And don't look at your watch. Give it what you want to give it and give it generously!

Two more points to make.

1. Don't overdo it. There is nothing worse than being a needy, clingy nuisance. It is possible to overdo it. And it will have a negative impact. Stop when it becomes "juicy." Just give yourself fully and completely for this short period.

2. Even if YOU think what you are doing is not working or having an impact, don't quit. Just as with earning points for your REA, give it your best without expectation (and in case you're wondering, these fifteen minutes *do not* earn you points). If you cut your time short with her because you believe it is not working, you will have done more damage than not spending time with her at all.

THE EMERGENCY BROADCAST SYSTEM

"This is a test. This is only a test. If this had been an actual emergency, the Attention Signal you just heard would have been followed by official information, news, or instructions."

The Emergency Broadcast System was established to provide the president of the United States with an expeditious method of communicating with the American public in the event of war, threat of war, or grave national crisis. It was later changed to deal with more domestic problems under the Federal Emergency Management Act (FEMA).

Women have their own EBS, and if you are married or in a relationship, you can rest assured that it has gone off more times than the nation's EBS system.

So, if you are like us, you hear the signal, focus your attention on the potential crisis, wait for instructions, and then execute those instructions. You have no control over what is being broadcast; you can only make decisions and be who you need to be based on the information given.

Most of the time, the instructions are "This was only a test, we now resume normal broadcasting."

So, 99.99 percent of the time the CONTENT of the EBS is a false alert—it was just a test. The alert itself is all that is important to you.

And 99.99 percent of the time the CONTENT of HER EBS is a false alert—it is just a test. The alert itself is all that is important to you.

If you really pay attention to your woman, you can see her EBS going off often, and how you deal with her distress signal will make all the difference in the relationship. Do the same thing you do when you hear it on the radio. Wait, Listen, Be Patient, and prepare for the response. You have no control over what she is going to say, only how you are going to be in reaction and respond to what she is saying, and what actions you are going to take in this particular crisis (that's when your FEMA system kicks in).

How do you react when her EBS is going off? Do you make up what she is feeling? Do you make her wrong for initiating her EBS? Do you predict what she going to say or feel next, and try to "fix" it before it happens? Do you ignore the alert altogether as some gigantic "cry wolf" game your woman is playing? Is it too difficult to wait for the instructions she wants to deliver? How many times have you missed an alert because you were not paying attention?

When a woman's EBS system is activated, all you need to do is sit up and take notice. Instructions are about to follow! Then what she says next might need to be translated.

Look at it like this: In addition to her day job and taking care of the emotional needs of the family, your woman has an important job to do. She must test you continually to keep you on your sharpest edge. It is her job. It is similar to the job teenagers have. Teens need to find out where their boundaries are—that's not bad, it's just their job. So they continually push and push the limits. If we go nuts on them, or give in because it's such a pain in the ass, we have failed them. All teenagers need to know is that they can go that far but no farther. Then they feel secure once again.

Your wife has to test limits too, because she is charged with the emotional well-being of the family, and she needs to keep you in shape. So she challenges you. It's a great thing—it's her job! She challenges your will and she challenges your terms. There are two kinds of tests: one kind to keep you sharp and one kind to make sure that you won't leave. These tests takes several forms, most of which fall into what we call the "do you love me now" test. Like "If I complain about being fat, will you still love me now?" "I am acting like a bitch, do you still love me now?" "I am withholding sex, do you still love me now?"

And the answer is and must always be: "I still love you." You have to be man enough, and secure enough in your own being to see these tests as a gift from your woman. We have said several times that it is not about you (and will throughout this guide) but this one is the hardest place in which to understand that. When your wife is upset, pointing at you, and saying "you (fill in the blank)," it is hard not to think that she is not talking about you. That is the test. When she is upset AT you, it is still her upsetness and it is about her (see the section on dealing with upsets—in section 5). Listen to her accusations from the perspective of the test. Is she feeling special, loved, unique, chosen, safe, and protected? Usually the accusation of your insensitivity or your dirty sweats on the floor (whatever) is just a test. Can you stand in and take the full brunt of her frontal assault? Can you listen fully to her rant? Can you let her cry and still see her as the magnificent creature you fell for so many years ago?

Your woman will also test you with her actions. She might be late coming home from work and not call you even though she asks you to call her if you are going to be late. Her doing this is also a test. Will you still love her even though she doesn't do something that she asks you to do? You may find that she may be giving you the "silent treatment." This can also be seen as a test. Will you still love her even though she is purposely avoiding talking to you?

Through all of this testing and seeming insecurity, you have to understand that she is just, absolutely perfect. The testing will make you stronger. Her different characters will make you more resilient and creative. Her moods will strengthen your character. It is exactly what you need and that is just perfect.

Every aspect of the EBS is a test to see if you love her in the state of emotion that she is in at that moment. Your answer should always be "yes" regardless of the situation. If you are to survive and be successful in your relationship with your woman, the answer is always "yes."

Rarely is it about what she is actually saying or what its content is. She is creating an opportunity for you to show that you love her. Just like the early days of the EBS, women run this test as often as they can. It could be because of insecurity, low self-esteem, or any other of a hundred things, but usually it is because she is "just checking." Such is a great woman who is always checking on the temperature of the relationship. It should be exciting for you, and you should have fun with it, and your answer, no matter how you word it, should always resemble "YES!" (Did we say that enough?)

Just don't ever make it about you, ever! If you are called on to do so, your natural FEMA manager will be ready, practiced, and alert.

Oh, and just in case you were wondering, the first two crises acted on by the newly created FEMA were "Love Canal" (the dumping of toxic waste in a local river) and the Three Mile Island "meltdown." Funny, huh? A meltdown and some toxins in the love supply. Nothing changes!

Survival Tip: "This was just a test. Had it been an actual alert, you would have been given instructions..."

SECTION 4

FIRE STARTERS

"Feel lust. Feel what it really is in its totality. Your lust reveals your real desire to unite with the feminine, to penetrate as deeply as possible, to receive her delicious light as food for your masculine soul, and to give her your entirety, losing yourself in the giving so that you are both liberated beyond your selves in the explosion of your gifts."

David Deida

Fire IS survival in the wilderness—providing warmth, light, and purification. But fire can also burn—you and the very forest you are in. The metaphor of passionate fire is one of the most common in the world of relationships. This section deals with the energy and power our differences create and the flames they can ignite.

(Kris and Dave)

THE PERFECT WOMAN

"I have only one itchin' desire: Let me stand next to your fire!"
Jimi Hendrix

OK, we've told you some of the ways men and women are different. And we've explained how these differences result in the most difficult challenges you face in your relationship with your woman. We've even given you some tools, and spelled out how you can develop a powerful way of being to help you deal with those challenges. Now it's time to go deeper, to get beyond dealing with problems, and develop an appreciation for your wife and your relationship with her that will take you from merely surviving to thriving.

Your wife is perfect—just the way she is. This idea may take getting used to especially if you find yourself in a "challenging" relationship. But the perfection of womankind is actually one of the operating contexts on which this guide is based. Each woman you have chosen throughout your life was exactly the right one for the time and place—she was perfect, even if later it turned out that the two of you grew in different directions and moved on. God does not create imperfection! Men's problems relating to women stem not from how crazy they sometimes seem, nor from their testing, trying, and nagging, but from the simple fact that they are not men. They do not think like men. They do not act like men. They do not decide like men. And thankfully they actually smell better than men!

So allow us to talk a little more about these divine creatures with whom we live, in the hope that we can convince you that they are, indeed, perfect. These observations don't necessarily apply to all women, and the last thing we want to do is to reinforce stereotypes, but we offer them because they have helped us to accept and appreciate our wives when we would otherwise be baffled and frustrated.

WOMEN ARE DIFFERENT (JUST IN CASE YOU HADN'T NOTICED YET)

As we have said, your wife is not from these parts. John Gray (the Mars and Venus guy) was right in that women are from another planet—he just got the planet wrong. They're actually from Krypton! Your wife is superhuman, and unless you deal with her as such, you run the risk of either being eaten alive or thrown out on your ear by someone half your size.

You want proof? First, let's talk about her superhuman powers:

<u>Multiple orgasms.</u> Face it—even when you were a teenager the best you ever could manage was to get it back up in fifteen minutes. But back-to-back like she can do? No way! And while we are at it...

<u>Faking orgasms.</u> Nope—splooge or no splooge—you just can't hide the truth, nor can you fake it. What—you think you can just spit on it or something? And if you're thinking she doesn't fake it now and then—get real!

If you think we're being silly or trite, let's consider such masculine territories as strength and pain. We have just three words for you: pregnancy, labor, childbirth.

<u>Pregnancy</u>. First of all, it would take a man a good five to ten years of hard drinking to develop a beer belly the size of a pregnant woman's—and she does that in nine short months! But, having done that, it would take that same man another ten years of disciplined training under some demonic, maniacal renegade from Paris Island to lose the belly he had built, but a woman loses it in a matter of hours. How she does it is further proof of her extraterrestrial power and strength.

<u>Labor.</u> (from Kris) Back in the day (remember the hippies?), I was helping my friends with the home birth of their son. Unfortunately for the mom, junior was lodged in there face forward—the wrong way. Now, at a hospital, they would just cut her open and take him, but we were at home. So the extraterrestrial woman in question went into what is called back labor—a process the Kryptonian body does to turn the fetus around. It is long and extremely painful, and the only relief is for the woman to be on her hands and knees while someone applies heavy pressure to her tailbone region. That is where I came in. Her husband and my wife stayed at the top end of this creature while I—for the next eight hours—applied back pressure. Repeatedly. Every minute, eight to ten times in a row, with about a three-minute break in between the cycles. *For eight hours* (did I say that?). To put a little more context to this, I am six three and two hundred thirty-five pounds, and at the time was a rugby player of fifteen years on a club and international level. I am no weakling. But by the time the baby was in delivery position, I was soaked with sweat and collapsed in semi-consciousness while the mom went on for two more hours of labor. That is not human! And though that was thirty years ago, and in the ensuing time I have hiked the Himalayas, climbed "the three thousand steps," run three Boston marathons, and broken multiple bones in athletic competition, I have never done anything that strenuous.

<u>Childbirth.</u> Consider this: try taking a baseball bat, greasing it up really good, and shoving it up your butt! No can do, eh? But that woman in question loses said belly by passing an object larger than the size of a rugby ball out through the orifice between her legs (yeah, we know, she told you that you were so big in there—right!). Now, you might want to consider the fact that doing so (passing the rugby ball) might be the source of just a little bit more pain than you have ever conceived of. See—they are extraterrestrials!

Survival Tip: Your woman possesses more skills and talents than you could possibly imagine. Don't try to compete or measure up. It is a waste of time for you and demeaning for her. Accept it and move on!

<u>Special Powers.</u> Besides their superhuman reproductive abilities, different women often have somewhat unique powers that betray them as aliens, although these may vary from specimen to specimen. For example, my wife has a memory worthy of a Cray supercomputer. Now, I know where my Leatherman Multitool, and perhaps the Makita Sawsall, are, but the list doesn't go much further than that. I can't find my favorite cufflinks, I have no idea where my Bruschi #54 sweatshirt is, haven't seen my 4-iron in two seasons, and couldn't find the key to the shed if my life depended on it.

Yet, one shout down the hall, "Honey, do you know where my (fill in the blank) is?" will confirm that the alien with whom I share my domicile is unquestionably of supernatural origin. Without hesitation comes the answer, "In the third drawer of the storage chest, on the left side just under the argyle sox Mom bought you that you never wear!"

I once got way down in the pile of grubbies that I keep around for nasty projects like painting or cleaning out the garage, and put on an old long-sleeve T-shirt. As I walked past my wife on the way to the project, she looked up from what she was doing, cocked her head to the side, and said, "Oh, that was the shirt you had on when you dumped me for Donna." I personally believe that her alien memory system works off some carbon-dated encoding power that she has. I could not tell you what I wore yesterday, but my wife can tell you exactly what I wore when I met her mother twenty years ago, and what day of the week it was (including the specific time). This is not human.

When you add these superhuman physical and mental powers to the fact that they speak a different language than men do (see "Listening" in section 3)—it's not hard to believe that women are extraterrestrials. And though we have tried to have a little fun with this, we really are trying to make a few important points:

1. Women are powerful in ways that men are not.
2. You are dealing with things beyond our understanding and you need some help. We all need a lot of help!
3. Women really are different from men—they are not just soft, good-smelling guys
4. Despite how hard it is to deal with these differences, they are just perfect!

And beyond these points, there are some other insights that we have gleaned and that have been given to us by our mentors. We offer these to help you accept and appreciate your wife, but with the caution that too much knowledge can be a dangerous thing, especially if you use it to analyze your wife or try to figure her out—that would just get in the way of loving her as she is.

Each woman is actually three women.

We believe that every woman has within her three elements. She is simultaneously a little girl, a queen, and a wild woman. Each woman has her own unique mix, and the mix changes from time to time (who knows why?), but it's helpful to appreciate this about your woman.

The Little Girl. There is a part of each woman's psyche that still needs to feel safe—the kind of safe she felt when she curled up on her daddy's lap. When she was little, Daddy made her feel safe. He was big and strong and provided everything her heart desired (generally speaking). Just like the playful boy in all of us men that never wants to grow up, this element of the female psyche never wants to leave the safety of Daddy's protection. Your job is to make her feel that safe and that secure. We already discussed this under the section on Men and Power (section 2). You need to make certain that her little girl part feels safe.

The Queen. This one is pretty apparent—your woman wants to be adored and placed on some kind of pedestal. She is the sovereign of the home and when the Queen is in the court, you are her humble guest. Adore her, bring her gifts. The Queen is the part of your woman that wishes that every day was her wedding day. The Queen loves it when the flowers you send to work are seen by everyone else—first—so that when she picks them up, everyone oohs and aahs. The Queen element is important especially when she is in the Court's presence (the presence of others). Ultimately what the Queen image boils down to is that you should never take your woman for granted—and that she should never feel common or taken for granted.

The Wild Woman. This is the trickiest of them all. Most men would think that a quote attributed to Queen Victoria is brilliant: "A woman should be a Lady in court and a whore in the bedroom." But the Wild Woman is not about sex (though some of the best sex you will have is with your wife's Wild Woman). The Wild Woman we're talking about is looking for the edgy, the dangerous, and the exciting. She wants to break all the goody-two-shoes rules she had to obey growing up as a girl. But she probably won't go there on her own—*you* need to invite the Wild Woman out to play. You do this by being the adventurer, the outlaw, the swashbuckling pirate—and not just in the fantasy sense, but in your life. You must be the Wild Man that your wife's Wild Woman would cheat on you for!

Case in point: a quick story from one of our men:

Like most men, Keith can't remember shit, and he let his driver's license expire. On top of that, he thought he had cleaned up an out-of-state ticket that he actually didn't, and was driving on a suspended license. While driving with his children a half mile from his home, he got pulled over by the local police who informed him of his dilemma, then decided to arrest him. He managed to get off a phone call to his wife who showed up almost instantly. She observed her husband in handcuffs, yelling at the police officer about how insulted he was about how he was being treated in front of his children. Keith was in such a furious rage, it took the officer five minutes to get him into the back of the cruiser.

Keith's wife was so turned on by her "outlaw" that he was not able to leave the bedroom for over a week! The moral of the story here is not that you need to get arrested, but that it is exciting for the Wild Woman when her man goes wild. It can be actually why women find James Bond, the ultimate bad boy, so attractive.

Now here is the other important thing to know about these basics: you never know who is waiting for you at the door. It may be the Little Girl or the Wild Woman—either way you need to be prepared.

One last thing you might want to know is that all of these references are in regard to the standard issue female. You know factory, floor models. We actually believe that there may be special models out there that are not like this and we think that they come in two classes:

The Deluxe Fantasy Model. Think of Mary—Cameron Diaz's role in *There's Something About Mary*. Here is a highly successful, well-paid professional pediatric specialist, whose favorite pastimes include things like getting a six-pack and going fishing or catching the Sox game on a whim. Then there is the Jane Smith model—as portrayed by Angelina Jolie in *Mr. & Mrs. Smith*—a drop-dead gorgeous sharpshooter who can kick the crap out of you and then screw your brains out without skipping a beat.

The Limited Edition, Volvo-Driving (Ex-Porn Queen) Soccer Mom. Thanks to Everclear for putting into lyrics our perennial question—where do all the ex-porn stars go? Our personal favorite was Jenna Jameson who is a PETA advocate and highly articulate speaker, with over one hundred hard-core movies that have a plot, excellent cinematography, and in which she actually delivers good lines. Unfortunately, she recently retired to give birth to twins and is living happily ever after with their father, MMA heavyweight champion Tito Ortiz. So get over her; you don't stand a chance!

That's it! That's all! If you have one of those special models you may not need to read any further. But all the rest—and we mean ALL the rest—are Factory Issue, Standard Models and that is what we are describing as the extraterrestrial, superhuman, unintelligible yet absolutely perfect creature with whom you are currently in relationship.

CHAMELEONS

Most people think that chameleons change color to blend in with their surroundings, but most chameleons actually use this ability to communicate social cues. Some chameleons let others know when they are ready to fight or to mate by moving pigments around in their skin cells to create dazzling and intricate displays of color. Some respond to changes in their environment or physiology with more subtle color changes.

With chameleons, as with many other species in the animal kingdom, it's the males who have adopted the more ostentatious displays of finery in order to attract mates and indicate their dominance. But curiously, modern (large corporate-based) human societies have subverted and suppressed what would naturally serve as a male dominance display—facial and body hair—and relegated this function to females in the form of elaborate and ever-changing hair styles, makeup, and clothing fashions. Maybe this is because women are more naturally adaptable and variable than men.

Guys see themselves fairly consistently and reinforce that with each pass in front of the mirror, flexing or sucking in the gut to be more in line with the perception. A woman is just the opposite, and the mirror can serve as a catalyst for changing her self-image. Of course, not every woman is a fashion maven or changes her hairstyle more often than men change their underwear. But we and other men we have talked to have noticed that the women in our lives have the wonderful and sometimes infuriating chameleon-like ability to change their moods and their minds based on their perceived needs of the moment, or sometimes for seemingly no reason at all.

As a result, living with a woman is like playing an extended game of Calvin-ball (from the cartoon *Calvin and Hobbes*, where Calvin continually changed the rules to fit his current circumstance). The general operating rules of a relationship are often in flux, because like Calvin, she changes the rules to suit her needs. Trying to keep up is futile, so beware: something you may think is right today could be wrong tomorrow. As we said earlier, your wife is continually testing you and challenging you to keep you at your best.

Of course, the constant testing can drive you crazy, and may remind you more of another master of adaptability in nature: *Plasmodium falciparum*,[33] the one-celled organism that causes malaria. It has so far been impossible to develop an effective vaccine for malaria because of its ability to adapt and change. Every time the human immune system tries to destroy it, it morphs and changes its surface to evade the attack. Scientists may one day develop an effective vaccine, but the effort has been hugely expensive, and there is little chance of financial return for the company that solves the problem. The analogy to marriage is apt, because if you choose to see your wife's changing the rules as challenging and testing as a plague that you have to fight against, you'll end up spending all of the relationship equity you build up (and more). Even if you could "win" in the end (which you can't), there's no return on your effort.

---

33 Thanks to our buddy, Dr. Bill Harris, the biophysicist, for the info!

But if you choose to see your wife the other way, as the mysterious and delightful chameleon that can change color on a whim, her morphing ability becomes just another one of her superhuman powers designed to sharpen your focus and hone *your* power. 'Nuff said!

BENEFITS OF COMMITTED RELATIONSHIPS

The dictionary defines benefit a few different ways, all of which are relevant to being in a long-term committed relationship.

The first definition is an "act of kindness." It is very important in a relationship that you are kind. Many times, you think you are kind or that you do "enough" for the relationship. But there is a different way of being kind with your woman. Kindness is a one-way street. You give it, and then give it some more, and give it again. And you give without any regard to what you may get in return. Selflessly. And it doesn't stop until you are dead. Anytime before that you are being selfish.

Giving without expectation is not a quality many men possess, but is a disciplined practice. You have to be constantly aware of the art of giving, and be conscious that there is no expectation on your part. If you give with expectation of something in return, you are bartering with your woman, and she will resent you for it. Why? Because she keeps score. Here is a well-known example of giving with expectation of something in return. We have all been there.

When was the last time you told your woman that you love her? Simply, "I love you." If it's heartfelt, and there's no expectation of getting an "I love you too" in return, then it's a gift. But when was the last time she didn't reciprocate, and you felt disappointed? You had an expectation, and your "I love you" was not a gift, it was a needy plea for reassurance. You can be sure that she was keeping score, and that you just lost REA points. Even if she reciprocated, she felt your neediness, and probably deducted even more points.

The second definition of benefit is "useful aid." In order for what you are doing to be useful, she needs to feel like it is helpful to her and the relationship. A great example is giving your wife a deep sensuous massage without the expectation of sex. Give that gift as a useful aid to the relationship and see what happens.

The third definition is "an entertainment function to raise funds for a certain cause." As we explained earlier in the section about the REA, the scoring system has been in place for as long as men and women have been together in relationships. The bad news is that it is as unpredictable as the stock market. You get to invest everything that you have, and sometimes you will score big, and sometimes you will lose big. More importantly, your woman's perception of you is like the stock market. One good day may positively affect the average a little but there must be a sustained uptick in order for the DOW to float upward. So because of that lack of predictability, you need to have a fundraiser occasionally. You need to go all out, like a weekend at the spa or a vacation alone; the sole purpose of

> I do my best to always thank my wife for or say something positive about anything she does for me, even routinely. I am not perfect, but often it's enough for her to know I care.

which is to raise funds for your cause. And the cause is to have the best of times with the woman that chose you to be her partner, for the rest of your lives.

The fourth and last definition of a benefit is "a *service* provided for an annuity, pension plan, or insurance policy." When you give selflessly to your wife, you are providing a service to the relationship. And by providing it instantly and creatively in the moment, you are building equity in the REA that will kick in and carry you when you start to slip, do something stupid, or when your woman decides for no particular reason to cash some of it in.

Now, somewhere in this discussion, it may have occurred to you that we have not talked at all about the benefits *you* receive from being in a committed, monogamous relationship. It's been all give, give, give, and that may seem like a raw deal for you. So why go through all of the work of the relationship? What benefits do you get if you give selflessly?

Your Benefits. Women are wonderful creatures. Without women in this world, men would probably just kill each other off. Without women, the world would be pretty black and white, cut and dried. Women provide Technicolor© perspectives. Women provide the security, love, and caring it takes to "domesticate" the animal in each man. Being in a relationship with a woman provides benefits to a man that he cannot get anywhere else. The first is a woman's love. It is beyond compare; without it, a man would most likely be an uncivilized beast, and he would never aspire to do more than fighting and killing. In tandem with that, love is the acceptance a man gets from his woman. This kind of love is huge for a man, and when it is given to him, as men's writers all the way from Robert Bly to Wayne Levine so often say,[34] it makes him believe he is better than he actually is. It can lift him up to a level where he is willing to take on the world. Only a wife can provide this and do so consistently.

---

34 Too many references to cite here.

Part of what lured you to marriage in the first place was the taste of that love when you were courting your wife. She tempted you by conjuring the feeling that you were better than you thought you were, and that feeling had you come back for more. It's a female mating ritual. And now that you're married, she will keep tempting you as long as she receives the benefit of you actually being a better man. Think about it: a woman feels good about you, she tempts you to be better, you become better, and she feels better about being with you. It's a perfect win for her and for you.

We note here that most women we know express love unconditionally only for their children. As one of our wives has so often said, she is certain that we can fend for ourselves, but she would throw herself in front of a bus to save her kid. The only unconditional love a man can ever experience comes from his mother. So you need to be clear that what you are seeking in your relationship is not simply a replacement for your mommy's love (that is a terrible thing to do to your wife). You have the right to expect unconditional love from your mother (whether you ever got it or not). But marriage is just a deal between two consenting adults: she makes you feel invincible; you go out and slay dragons; she admires you and feels safe enough to repeat the cycle. Love and acceptance from your wife is not unconditional in the way your mother's love was. However, when you provide your benefits unconditionally, it provides the space for her to be able to provide her love and acceptance for you. (We'll pause for a moment of silence in honor of all the romantic fairy tales that may have suffered irreparable damage in this paragraph.)

Another major benefit of the committed life is being a father. Children provide a man with both a legacy that can be carried on, and a connection to something bigger than himself. They provide an instantaneous higher purpose—they connect you to the future (their future) through your teaching and training. As a father, you teach your son how to be a man and you teach your daughter what a committed man looks like so that she can spot one for herself in later years.

Beyond all of these benefits, marriage to your one and only woman gives you access to out-of-body experiences that can only be described as priceless, such as your wedding day, your children's births, your first house. Only when you have committed to being the foundation for the life that you have created together do these things happen in just the way that holds you together. And they just start appearing as long as you stay in there as a committed force. Sometimes they are just fleeting moments, like the look in her eyes when you give her your best, you listen, and you are there for her in good times and bad. Sometimes they seem to last forever, like when it feels as if there is nothing else in the world except you and her.

But the bonus in the deal that a committed relationship provides is a sense of hope – yea hope (we all could use that!). Seriously, the benefit of the relationship is that as a couple we actually are more complete, more capable and more wonderful that either of us are on our own. That does not mean that you get to come to the relationship with any less that one hundred percent of your full being, it just means that as humans we somehow get that we were meant to be together and that there is some synergism about that we can access. It is actually a benefit enjoyed by both parties of the relationship.

The truth is, you don't need a relationship to satisfy your basic needs: a few toys, a good orgasm now and then, your own place—hey, men are pretty simple creatures. But you, like most other men, want it all, and the love of a woman, along with those priceless experiences of family life, and the glimmer of hope that you can actually create something together are the main reasons we all are here. OK, enough of the sappy schmaltz—back to reality!

Survival Tip: Men are consistent and women are dynamic and mutable. *Vive la difference.* Expect your woman to be many different women and start enjoying all of them. After all, we men love variety!

SEX

"Now some they do and some they don't and some you just can't tell.
And some they will and some they won't and some it's just as well."

Supertramp

I f you're in one of those relationships where you enjoy a healthy
supply of good, steady sex with your wife, congratulations! But
for many couples, there is a difference in the partners' rhythms
and appetites for sex, and at times it can become flat and obligatory,
or dry up altogether. Our purpose here is to show you how the
lessons in this book relate to the sexual aspect of your relationship,
and how applying them can revitalize your sex life.

It has long been said that men get to intimacy through sex and
women get to sex through intimacy. Did you notice that when we
talked about the differences between men and women earlier, we
didn't mention sex? Well, here's that conversation.

Men are fueled by the quest for sex

Remember back to the time before you were married, when you were pursuing a woman you were unbearably hot for—maybe your wife, maybe not. What did it feel like when you were in the hunt, and then when you finally got her? That's what we're talking about here—that all-consuming drive that forces you to sweep away all obstacles between you and your prey, and then, when you get her, fills you up with the juice that would make you take on the attacking Huns single-handedly. Chances are, the woman in question did not have those feelings—who knows what she was feeling, but not that. Even now, you may get that feeling after a great session with your wife.

Women are not fueled by sex.

Some may like it, others even love it. To some it occurs as some kind of duty or chore they must perform, while to others it is fun and delightfully enjoyable. But for most women, sex must be linked to safety, intimacy, love, and respect for it to be a sustaining force in the relationship. And the relationship is always her main concern, so sex is more of a means to an end, rather than the end itself, as it is for men.

Here lies the issue of the century. Men are fueled by sex and excited by the quest for sex, and woman simply are not. This creates a unique environment for marriage survival. Now, if your woman gave you sex without you having to work for it, it would probably lose all value and you would quickly turn into a lazy fat sloth whose only purpose was to figure out a way to keep your dick hard. It's the thrill of the hunt that keeps you engaged and at your best. And the extent to which that drive makes you a powerful, loving man is the extent to which your wife will feel safe, protected, loved, and respected, which creates the intimacy that makes her want you. But before you get too excited, let us say a bit about sex itself. There are many kinds and qualities of sex for men, only a few of which will benefit the relationship.

First there is hormonal sex. This is the acting out of your inner teenager. As a teen, you were assaulted by an explosion of testosterone that coursed through your bloodstream, causing random erections, wet dreams, and uncontrollable desires. Whether these urges are acted on or left unfulfilled, hormonal sex drives, when they enter into the space of the marriage relationship, have nothing to do with your wife—they are only about you and your wants and perceived needs. Even if your wife enjoys it and has multiple orgasms, if *your* focus is getting your rocks off, she will sense it. Sex that is for you does not nourish the relationship, which is *her* focus, and she will count it as a withdrawal from the REA.

An advanced form of hormonal sex is the therapeutic fuck (TF). The TF is an intense and physical bout of sex that is hormonally driven, but occurs more like the alpha male ravishing his female.

Recently I went to India and they took me to the Temple of Wisdom, and it was a hundred feet high and it was carved all over with all the stories of the Kama Sutra — and it is all there — everything you could possibly imagine and some you couldn't — there are no new things in sex or relationships!

If not engaged in mutually, the TF is actually hurtful and violating, but when both partners get into their roles, the TF is a passionate, powerful, and physical dance of the sexes that leaves both participants weak in the knees. This is the kind of sex that is depicted most often in pornography, where the woman is overwhelmed by the power of the sexual experience and loses all control and inhibitions. Nice! But caution must be taken to ensure that you are both on the same plane. Most of the time, the pornographic version of sex is a fantasy made up by overly hopeful male filmmakers wishing all women were whores (the root *porno* is Greek for "harlot"), which is why it is called pornography.

Adventure sex and fantasy sex are both residuals of your single life. For men, sex as a single man is an adventure in exploration—

sights and sounds and smells. Each woman does it differently and reacts to your chase differently. This is intoxicating and habit forming, and generally, like the TF, can be an exciting spice to add to the marriage but must be engaged in by invitation and mutual consent, lest it backfire on you. A good way to meet your need is to set up a date and to engage in a "pretend" session. Test out some ideas first to learn her appetite for fantasy. Again, if this in any way sounds to her like it's about you, she can perceive it as not wanting her as she is. If you make it about inviting her out to play—about inviting her inner Wild Woman to come out and to break her rules, it can be exciting, exhilarating, and fueling for the relationship.

In each of the above, the key issue is that when the sex is about you, it is not contributing to the relationship, and, in fact, may detract from it. Your woman experiences sex as one of two kinds: sex for you and sex for her (and the relationship). Many forms of sex amount to nothing more than husbands using their wives for masturbation.

But this doesn't mean that sex must be about her all the time. It's OK to ask for sex (and when you ask, it's obviously for you). But when you do, you must make room in the question for her to say no, and if she does, don't make it a problem. There may even be times when she does not want sex, doesn't have the least interest in having an orgasm, yet may still be willing to be a full participant as a favor to you or in exchange for a great backrub later on, or simply because she loves you and cares.

Oh, and lest we forget, asking continually is counter-productive, and whining or bitching about the lack of sex is right out. The truth is, if you are not having enough sex, look at how you are being in the relationship, not at your wife's frigidity! So you get horny! Get over it! First of all, despite teenage myths to the contrary, there are no such things as blue balls or toxic sperm buildup! You are just horny. When you're in a sex drought the first place you need to look is at yourself and your way of being. Is it possible you are focusing on your neediness? Hey, we said at the outset that this was not going to be a party and that you may not like all of the pointers. Well here's one. If you are experiencing a lack of sex, then it is likely that you are being a needy, whining little boy, concerned only about self-satisfaction and where you might be getting your next blow job! Well, simply put—cut it out. Start there and figure the rest out.

Did that just offend you or piss you off and make you want to throw this book in the trash? Well, sometimes it takes a slap in the face to get someone to admit to an uncomfortable truth about himself. And in our experience over the years coaching men, we've run into many who are totally unaware of the sometimes subtle ways that their immaturity shows up in their relationships (and not just with their wives). So if you were offended, chances are it's because we hit a sore spot, and you would be doing yourself, and your wife, a favor by looking inside and being honest with yourself about how that needy little boy sometimes runs the show. And it helps to take it to your men, which is the one place that you can, and should open up about these things.

So how do you have sex that fuels the relationship? Rule #1: A woman's primary sexual organ is her mind. If you fail to engage that, you are facing an uphill battle. I don't know if we even have to say this, but if she initiates the subject, never turn her down! It means her mind is already in the game. Your job, however, is not to oblige with a wham-bam-thankya-ma'am, but rather to respond by asking her what she would like (further engaging that primary organ). Get her in the habit of being explicit in her requests, both general (I want a long languid lovemaking session) and specific (a little harder, there!). Just as women generally have a far better emotional vocabulary than men do, our experience tells us that they also have a better classification system for what constitutes good sexual arousal for them. For us, sex is like ice cream—even plain vanilla is good! Your assignment is to find out by asking, and asking again, and asking again—every time. There is no Rule #2.

The old adage we referenced before, that men get to intimacy through sex and women get to sex through intimacy, is often heard by men as a big problem—now they need to learn how to be intimate. Not really (and this is key) you only need to learn how to provide the space and conditions for your *wife* to become intimate. It is she who needs the intimacy in order to become sexually engaged. So the question becomes what can you can do to create a safe haven in which your woman can open up and become intimate? The answer is the same things that are discussed repeatedly throughout this guide. Let's review some that are on the short list:

- **Your strength and protection** are primary in this arena. Make sure she feels safe and secure.
- **Listening** is a critical element of creating intimacy for her. Listen to what she says and listen to what she does not say. Listen to what she means as much as to what she says. Get good at listening.
- **Not fighting and disagreeing**—this is not being a "yes, dear" kind of wimp! It is your recognition that winning arguments, competing with her, and being right have no place in sustaining the relationship. Compete with other men; cooperate and compromise with your wife.
- **Provide focused, uninterrupted attention**—with no distractions from work, phone, kids, or TV. Fifteen minutes of focused, uninterrupted time with her each day may be sufficient. And next time you find yourself surfing the net, stop, turn off the computer and go focus on her (same for porn, vegging out, or any other distraction that isn't your personal, reflective/refueling time). Remember, building and maintaining a successful relationship is a discipline.

There is a great book that just came out on this which should make its way to your bookshelf. Buy a copy of the Hallowell's *Married to Distraction* – there are literally hundreds of good tips on this topic.[35]

- And finally, **be the man she would cheat on you with**. At some point in your courtship, your woman found you to be irresistible. Maybe she couldn't keep her eyes or hands off of you. Remember what you were like back then—odds are you were powerful: you were fit and active, or successful in your business or job, or a leader around the town or at church; intensively alive in some way. If you have stopped being powerful, she probably isn't as attracted to you. *The very best thing you can do for your woman's sex appetite is to work on yourself.* Practice your disciplines of fitness, effectiveness, decisiveness, spirituality, and most of all, your courtship disciplines. Remember that what got her to have sex with you the first time was that you actively courted her—maybe even seduced her—by continually focusing your best efforts on her and what would please her. If you are doing any less now, you have gotten lazy in your relationship, and you can expect a lowered response from her.

That's all we're going to say about sex. There are writers who are far more experienced and articulate in the department of sex relationships than we are, and we know how and when to step aside and let a master talk. Deida[36] teaches a set of skills that elevate sex from a stupid biological function, not much more elaborate than eating and defecating, to an art form to be mastered! We refer you to the several books and workshops by David Deida on the topic (*Intimate Communion, Finding God Through Sex, Blue Truth,* and *Dear Lover*

---

35 Complete citation in the References section.

36 Complete citation in the References section.

(for your wife) along with our perennial recommendation, *The Way of the Superior Man*). Also, try getting a copy of a little book called *Romantic Fantasies* by Gregory Godek and read it together with your wife. It has a bunch of fun and intriguing ideas.*

Oh, and don't forget—have fun!

> ***Survival Tip:*** Make sex about her—the more you focus on her needs, in foreplay, during sex and in "afterplay," the more she can and will surrender to you.

---

* Full reference is included in the works cited section at the end of the book.

SOME BIGGER (AND MORE ADVANCED) DIFFERENCES

All of the differences explained in the last few sections stem from the understanding that women are emotionally based creatures. They say and do everything from their current emotional state. Their emotional state can change every second, or linger for days. Women bond with each other around this essential aspect of femininity. They come together to assist each other in processing these changing dynamics in complex and (what we men might consider, obtuse) ways. It is the foundation of a relationship. It is very hard for a man to understand this, and is why most men either run away when emotions are high, or say some stupid, dumbass thing that just makes it worse.

Men are problem solvers—The Antichrists of a relationship. We think everything can be solved. Actually, we *can* solve everything—and most often (we think) by ourselves. Some of it blows up in our faces, and some of it works. That isn't the point. In fact, in this guide, we assert that it is important to suppress this urge sometimes, and just listen to your woman. Your woman's "problems" don't need to be "solved." She is trying to relate to/with you when she tells you about them and you destroy the potential of bonding when you make that go away.

So why do you actually care if you have a relationship with a woman that is actually better than the man standing next to you? Said differently, you actually can float through life, be mediocre, have no aspirations, or even worse yet, think that this is the best it is ever going to get. You care because deep down inside your gut, you are disappointed. You wish it could be better. You keep hoping it could be better. You wake up and tiptoe around, hoping the unleashing of your woman's emotional fury and wrath will not be aimed at you or anything you care about. We've got to admit, sometimes it works. But it is like jury duty. You know that someday, somewhere, somehow, you are going to get picked. And when you do, you are going to be pissed. And most likely you will take the same attitude. Why did I get picked? Of all the people in the world, why me? This is the wrong time for this to happen. Shouldn't it be someone else's turn? Couldn't this just go away and never come back?

The great thing about jury duty is you can't get out of it. If you try to squiggle out of it, there is a cost. And the government has set the cost high enough that you will actually perform the duty required of you.

Being in a relationship is the same way. As with jury duty, you have a choice. You can actually just pay the price for not doing your part. But as with the court system, the costs of not stepping up to your duty are high. Living a miserable to mediocre life is certainly one of them. Another is that the relationship never flourishes and neither party receives any benefit from it. And perhaps worst of all is that the relationship dies. It certainly sounds foolish to invest the time, caring, and love at the start of the relationship, and then ignore it until it becomes a problem, halfheartedly do something about it, and then repeat the process all over again, and again, and again. If you are not truly committed to the relationship, give it a merciful death. Grow up and face the truth. You are not willing to do the work and you shouldn't deprive your woman the opportunity to have a man who is actually willing to do it. By the way, this is one of the major reasons why there are so many single women on this planet. It is not because there are not enough men; it is because there are not enough men who are willing to practice the discipline of being in a relationship.

SECTION 5

FIRST AID

"Wars are won by breaking the will of your enemy to fight on. To fight and conquer in all battles is not supreme excellence. Supreme excellence consists of breaking the enemy's resistance without fighting."

Sun Tzu

I n the wild, small wounds can become big setbacks if not treated quickly and effectively. In marriage, the little hurts build up just as quickly. This section deals with some basic but indispensable remedies.

(Kris and Dave)

WHEN LISTENING DOESN'T WORK

"My husband and I have never considered divorce...
murder sometimes, but never divorce."
Dr. Joyce Brothers

Sometimes you've done your best to listen and it hasn't worked. Sometimes your woman, no matter how great you are, no matter how much you are listening, is just not ready to move from the place or emotion she is in. So what do you do?

Play dumb—not because you can, but because you are.

As we just said, men are problem solvers by nature, but most of the time you don't need to solve your woman's problems. You just need to lend a listening ear. There is a trick to lending a listening ear, and it can take on many different forms; however, it all must come from the same place: playing dumb—listening as if you know nothing. In Eastern philosophy, this is referred to as "beginner's mind," but we just call it playing dumb. *Pretend* that you don't know what she is talking about, even if you think you do. And we say "think," because in your human male mind, your ego has you believe that you know what she is thinking or talking about. The best way to succeed in the relationship and make her happy is to play dumb. We could cite thousands of examples, but one should suffice. You have to trust us on this one, but it should make sense coming from one dumb guy to another.

Your wife asks you "Do you think I look fat?" What do you say? Here are some "smart" answers, and we strongly suggest that you never use any of them:

You have put on a couple of pounds since we first met.
Only around your ass and thighs.
Yeah, but look at your mother.
Don't worry, it's only about twenty pounds.
In today's society, it is hard to stay thin and trim.
An exercise class would take care of that.
Thighmasters are on sale this week—want me to get you one?
A woman that has handles really turns me on!
Define fat, honey.

This is a trap! And the only way not to get sprung in the trap is to play dumb. However here are a few "dumb" answers that just might save your ass!

Huh?
I don't understand what you're talking about.
I love you very much.
You're not fat; you're just having a bad dream.
Cut it out.

We hope you get the idea. There are many times in a relationship that playing dumb will save your ass. Don't get wrapped up in problem solving.

Now, there are times that you need to problem solve. If your wife is trying to fix a leaky sink, and is having a tough time with that, you should step in and fix the sink. Really—it might be better for you to do that if you know how.

You are probably good at doing a few other things, by the way. Try to stay in the areas you are qualified in. Stake out your territory and stick to it. Here is a typical list that most men can lay claim to:

Lift and move objects, especially heavy ones.

Fix broken inanimate objects.

Drive a car, and parallel park it in a tight spot.

Take out the trash and perform other household duties.

Build shit.

Demolish (tear shit down).

That's it. Now of course some of you may be skilled at doing the taxes (we're split 50/50—one of us being great at it and the other still trying to figure out why he has to pay taxes anyway) or cooking (again split here with us, only the other way) or whatever. And it might be added that there are some issues—specifically parenting—that are and must be joint partnerships (see the section called "And Baby Makes Three"). But everything else about the relationship and the art of relating, and we mean *everything* else, most of us are not really expert at doing. When asked about anything else other than your specific mastery items, PLAY DUMB AND JUST LISTEN!

It is really hard to stay focused in these situations. At the time of this writing, Dave had been married for twenty years. To this day, when his wife wants to be listened to, he says his pea brain still believes that he can fix her problem. At least fifty percent of the time, he walks into the trap. Later, after he has sewn his leg back on, he laughs at it all, but in the moment, he just takes the bait hook, line, and sinker. We will say more about this in the section on "Pushing Your Buttons."

Hey, if you want to fix something when your woman wants to talk, fix your ears and fix your urge to do anything other than listen. Fix your listening on her and just be present with her.

HAVING THE LAST WORD—ARGUMENTS AND FIGHTING

I t is our bet that the last time someone talked to you about fighting was in the schoolyard in middle school. Certainly, prior to marriage, you and your blushing bride did not sit down and discuss how you would disagree, and certainly, you didn't use the word fighting, despite the fact that you may have fought, bickered, or even broken up before or during the engagement. So let's talk about that now.[37]

There is a difference between disagreeing and fighting. When you two disagree, there is a built-in allowance that the other person has a different point that is (perhaps) worth considering. But in a fight, you get positioned. And, what's worse, you run the risk of doing some serious damage by using the "Four Horsemen of the Apocalypse" in fighting. In fighting, we men tend to revert to defensiveness, sarcasm, criticism, or stonewalling.

---

37 With a little guidance from J.M. Gottman, *What Predicts Divorce?* Lawrence Earlbaum, Hillsdale, NJ, 1994.

<u>Defensiveness</u> is most often a man's first line in fighting. Because we feel at times we are on foreign soil (after all, relationship is not an area we are well schooled in), we take a defensive stance when she pulls out the guns in attack. This is not denial ("Hey, I didn't do anything!") but can be either justification ("Look, I am trying to be reasonable here.") or counterattack ("Well, now you know how pissed I was when you dressed me down in front of our neighbors yesterday."). Defensiveness is a reaction of your whining "little boy" and is a cue for you to shut up and start listening. Defensiveness is a quick-twitch reaction that is easily controlled by listening.

<u>Sarcasm</u> is a form of disrespect that cuts deep in relationship. Most often, sarcasm is a salvo aimed at her self-esteem and it is meant to hurt! Ranging from rolling your eyes (especially in public) to below-the-belt smacks ("Ooo, that was mature!"), sarcasm can slip into a fight without a moment's notice. The remedy is just as quick, however. When you catch your dark sarcasm popping up follow it with some form of admiration or affirmation—as quickly as you can. Or simply throw in an admission that you may not have done any better ("Actually, that was pretty good; I don't know if I could have managed as well!")

<u>Criticism</u>, as opposed to sarcasm, is aimed at making your wife wrong. Criticism has two forms: one is the use of nasty labels (selfish, bitch, and the "c-word" women take most offense to), and the other is generalizing ("you always/ never"). The easiest thing to do when you find yourself wanting to criticize is to use the first person singular. Instead of accusing with "you," identify with "I" ("I think we ought to…"). Another tactic to adopt is what we call "causing right." Instead of making her wrong, try focusing on causing the "right" thing to happen. How can you steer the conversation in a different direction by asking a question?

Stonewalling is a mainly masculine form of fighting and ranges from just walking out (to avoid becoming violent) to clenched-teeth silence. We were told not to fight with girls when we were younger, so when that old lesson pops up, we shut down. When you find yourself shutting up or shutting down, force yourself to ask a clarifying question ("Help me understand" or "What do you mean?"). And by the way, women stonewall us too (we tend to refer to it as the cold shoulder) and even have a few more tools in the stonewalling kit than we do—Did you ever get the skinny-eyed, pursed lip treatment? Has she ever withheld sex as stonewalling? When she does that, just stay with her, and even let her know verbally that you aren't going anywhere; you can wait until she is ready to talk. By the way, you can (and at times, should) walk away from a fight. Just be sure to tell her that you need to get a breath of air or time to collect your thoughts while doing something, but that you will come back and finish discussing the topic.

There is one more important piece to this. Apologize. Tell her you're sorry. We recommend that you don't try to explain why you did whatever it was that set her off (or you as the case may be)—that is just being defensive again! Explaining can just serve to make the conversation about you again. But let's be clear: we are not asking you to be a wimp or a "yes, dear" man. A powerful, loving man can apologize for anything, even if to him it is not true. Apology is a form of acknowledgement for a woman. Be sincere; try really being sorry—not necessarily for what you did, but for the fact that she is upset—just say, simply, "I'm sorry." Take what she has to give to you, and love her through it. A woman loves being in an environment where she can be however she needs to be and do whatever she needs to do to express her emotions fully. It is up to you to provide this safe space.

If you do this, she will love you. She will talk about you to her friends. She will give you what you want. She will put you on a pedestal. And then, when you are starting to feel good about the whole thing, she will start it all over again (because after all, you made it safe for her to be). This is one of the signs of a high-quality, wonderful woman. This type of woman is a keeper!

One last thing: the world out there (outside of your house) is yours. Go get it, Tiger! Compete all you want; score big points, and bring home the spoils to your family. But whatever you do, keep your competitiveness and the need to make it about you (if you really must) out there. It has no place in your relationship with your wife.

DEALING WITH YOUR WIFE'S "FINE" (UPSETS)

There are times when it seems there is a large flashing sign above your woman's head that says "I'M UPSET WITH YOU!" But when you (rather stupidly) ask if anything is wrong she tells you she's "fine." It may feel like a stiff arm from a Heisman Trophy-winning running back, but it is simply a notification that she is "Feeling Intense Negative Emotions," and it might be handy for you to stick around.

But what to do? Allow us to break it down for you. First of all, contrary to TV sitcoms and pop psychology, the man is not always wrong, so no head-down, tail-tucking behavior on your part. Worry less about being in the wrong—even when or if you have screwed up (and you will)—and instead stay focused on keeping your feet under you and your wits about you. It may help to focus more on things as only worked/didn't work and get back in there. The best course is to try to understand what the nature of the upset is that your woman is feeling, then to stand in there and deal with it like the man you are.

There are three major reasons why she might be upset, and there are logical, proven ways of dealing with each.

Upset #1: Misaligned or violated expectations

First of all, you need to understand that I, you, and every other human on the planet (except perhaps for some highly advanced Buddhist monks) live in a world created by our own expectations. Simply put, most people rarely stay in the present moment, preferring instead to think about what is coming next. The result of thinking of the next thing (and the many nexts after that) is that we build up a set of expectations about how this or that—or life in general—is going to be. That is normal and human. Girls start practicing this art (with respect to relationships) at an early age (Seriously, did *you* sit around with your buddies fantasizing about your wedding when you were ten?), so they are much further down the path in having expectations about relationships than men. But this is only half the issue. The other and more important part is that you and she likely have never discussed your expectations.

So the problem becomes that you have one expectation: "It's Saturday. I think I'll wash the car and get a six-pack so Jimmy and I can watch the BC-Notre Dame game." She, on the other hand, has a different expectation: "Since it is a nonwork day for you, and you have nothing special planned, you can help me with the gardening." Admittedly a rather trite or simplistic example, but the point is neither of you has discussed these expectations with the other, so when you do not show up to fulfill hers, she is upset, and so are you when she confronts you.

Let me give you a BIG example of how this works. On Tuesday, September 11, 2001, Kris woke up to a bright blue, crispy clear September morning and expected it to be a great day. He was running day two of a workshop for a client company and expected it to go as well as the first day had gone. And then some crazy maniacs decided to fly planes into buildings and, no surprise, he got really upset (along with the rest of the nation). We are not making light of 9/11, but ask you: what were your expectations that were violated that day? Did you have the expectation of safety in America; that no one would hate America so much that they would do that; that our early warning systems, our national intelligence network, and our superior military could never let such a thing happen? Or did you have a brother in the building, and just assumed that you would always have the chance to see him again? Violated expectations are that big! And the emotions that come with a violated set of expectations can be immense.

Dealing with Upset #1

If just listening fails to diffuse your wife's upset, assume first that she has an expectation of you that was not met. The next step is simple: just ask, "Wow, it's clear that you expected me to do something that I haven't done. What was that?" Now, you do not have to fulfill all of her expectations, some of which may be unreasonable. The key is to get them out on the table alongside your expectations and talk them through, because by that point, it's obvious that you simply have not had the expectations conversation. This applies to both big expectations ("I want to have another baby.") and smaller ones ("I thought you were going to fix the dishwasher."). The big ones are the trickiest, because, like most couples, you probably discussed your expectations around these long ago when you were first married or engaged, with the unspoken assumption, "I'll let you know if anything changes!" Well, stuff changed—little by little, imperceptibly—and neither of you noticed. But like a slight one-degree rotation of your golf grip puts you in the weeds two hundred yards out from the tee, a little change here and there makes a radical difference in ten or fifteen years.

There is a cartoon of a bride and groom kneeling at the altar with a little thought bubble above each head. Above the man it says, "Thank you, God, at last I can count on having good, safe, steady sex." Above the bride's head the bubble reads, "Thank God I never have to give another blow job in my life!" Men might give a little chuckle at that cartoon (neither of us even think it is funny!), but women seem to find it hysterically funny! It's all about expectations.

Upset #2: Loss of voice

The second major source of pain and upset is another natural human need that is amplified for women. As humans, we all need to be heard. We need to know that our voice has counted for something and that we are recognized as having made a contribution to the thought process. When we have not been asked for our input, or when we have not even been invited to the discussion table, it upsets us. This is especially true when it comes to matters affecting us, like our jobs, our pay, or our families. Now take that naturally occurring need and place it inside a woman in a marriage relationship. Though it may border on sexist to say that women are better talkers, remember that you and your buddy can go fishing and not say more than three sentences all day and you think it was deeply bonding. Women talk to bond and therefore are not only more practiced and accomplished at the conversational arts, they need to have their voices heard—by you—their husbands.

It is important to distinguish the "loss of voice" upset from the kind she feels because of unmet expectations. Loss of voice means that you haven't asked her opinion on an issue that is important to her. Remember that, as Deborah Tannen tells us, a woman gets into a relationship through discourse, so she feels that if this is a "partnership," then you should have sought her opinion. You, on the other hand, are a man of action and, seeing a problem, need no further input to just spring into action. It is the Warrior's way. And that's probably a big reason why she married you in the first place: your action and problem-solving prowess made her feel safe and protected. But now you are together in a relationship and that requires talking—her talking. So when you do not ask for her opinion, her input, or her feelings on a subject that is important to her, she loses her "voice" in the relationship (which is the very essence of relationship for her)... and... she gets... upset!

Just as important as asking for her opinion is listening to it and incorporating it into your action. Having a voice in the matter often translates to having been listened to. If you learn nothing else from this guide, we hope that you get the message to become a great, actively engaged, high-quality listener. In other words, the implications of Tannen's research and her assertion that "talking is for girls and women" is that we do not have to be skillful conversationalists. All we have to be is willing listeners. Is that so much to ask?

Dealing with upset #2

The best way to deal with the loss of voice upset is to prevent it by knowing when you need to get her input, and then asking for it. And you need to know when you should incorporate her feedback into what you are doing (and when you don't need to).

Asking can be done in a hundred different ways and it would be to your advantage to create some for yourself. If you are not terribly accomplished at discussion starters (like if you find yourself out on a dinner date with her and you quickly run out of things to ask or say), start by brainstorming with your men to produce a set of good opinion-seeking questions. You should target a list of no less than ten good ones that you then commit to memory. Practice using them—over dinners out. You know, the times when you are at a restaurant and you just want to talk sports or about how good the meal is. Instead, try asking one of your opinion-seeking questions. Find out which feel good saying them, or which get the best responses from her and file them away to use later.

But listening is just as important as asking for her opinion. Remember, we are not talking about the Listening 101 stuff of eye contact and reflection—that's nice but not varsity. Intense listening, as we have described, listens to the source of the speaking—to the "why" behind "what" she is saying. You want to listen for the commitments and values that must be operating in order for her to say what she said. For example, we were once on a panel of men invited to answer some serious questions about marriage from participants at a women's workshop. One woman stood up and asked how to deal with her husband who didn't want to do a particular thing. One of our crew replied, "Well, I think I heard your question, but it sure sounds like there is something much more serious going on; why don't you ask us what you really want to know?" And the tears just flowed out as she described a really tough encounter complicated by her husband's long-term family dynamics. That woman left the workshop feeling as though she had a voice that we actually heard, and we were certain her marriage life would be significantly impacted as well.

Upset #3—Lack of movement

Again, one of those normal human needs comes to the forefront in this upset. Humans are growing, evolving beings that need to have a sense of that growth and freedom to move in order to maintain sanity. Many people (both men and women) have a vague discomfort and dissatisfaction with their lives, and don't realize that it's caused by a lack of movement. They try to change trivial things, like getting in shape, or buying a sports car, or having an affair, or taking Prozac, until they hit bottom when nothing relieves that itch. Then they realize that their lives are stagnant in a more meaningful sense, and start to move in a more meaningful and satisfying way. That's why it may look to the casual observer (the JV listener) that she just wants to keep up with the Joneses, or with Oprah. But give her more credit than that—she's going through her process. And maybe the reader can help his wife if he listens to what is behind her actions and words.

The deepest form of this upset is feeling trapped. Being confined in a space smaller than you are, in which you can neither fully stretch out nor stand up, as the VC practiced in the Vietnam War, is pure torture. Feeling trapped is the worst version of the loss of movement and, believe it or not, that can easily occur in a marriage relationship.

When your wife feels her life is not moving anywhere, the feeling is suffocating. Now the problem with all of this is that she will tell you that what she really wants more than anything is stability. This is not to be confused with the lack of movement, growth, and increasing status/respect, all of which are dynamic forces. So the trick you have to mastermind is to allow wide enough berth in the life you two are creating, while providing a measure of predictable stability to it!

No easy task.

Once again, as we cautioned with voice, do not confuse this with an expectation. Movement is very specific and has everything to do with personal, psychological, and emotional development. Worse yet is that this apparent lack of movement is often relative to other objects and personalities around her. It can come as a result of not moving at the same rate or developing as rapidly or faster than any other relative objects (read this as her friends, or Oprah's standards, or whatever happens to be in pop literature at the moment).

Dealing with Upset #3

The good news is that she is the source of both the interpretation of the issues and the movement. So in truth, you do not have to create actual movement (we know one guy who put his house on the market, packed up the family, and moved across the country to satisfy his wife's itch to move toward her dream. While that is admirable, it is not necessary—most of the time). The first piece of coaching is stay away from issues concerning weight and health (that is not movement or "growth"). Instead, this skill takes paying attention to her dreams and aspirations. Notice her artifacts. If she scrapbooks or makes dream posters, study them and if you want to be a real hero, put some of what is in them into play. Kris' wife was building a preschool a few years ago and the process was going to be long and time consuming before she would actually realize her dream. So he went to the property and found a boulder (about eight inches in diameter), engraved it with her vision statement, and then gold leafed and polyurethaned it as a gift that eventually was placed in her office when the building was opened up. But for the four years of pre-opening work, it represented for her the very real movement toward her dream. Movement is all about her dreams.

A Last Word on Upsets

When your woman is upset it is imperative that you allow her to have her emotions. Most of the time that means standing there and listening to it spew out at you. Just listen—that's often all you have to do. And keep listening—despite the temptation to do so, do not ask, "Are you done?" Bad idea!

If just listening isn't enough, know that one of the above three upsets is in play and act accordingly. But there is one other case we need to explore.

Survival Tip: Your wife's upset is not yours. Practice keeping perspective and know what is hers and yours. That way you can be conscious enough to respond appropriately.

A Woman's Rage

Let's make a quick distinction between "upset-ness" and RAGE. It was written (and often attributed to the bard, Shakespeare himself, but in truth comes from a play called *The Mourning Bride*), "Heaven hath no rage like love to hatred turned, *nor hell a fury like that of a woman scorned.*" Women are capable of incomprehensible levels of rage and if that is turned toward you, and despite our encouragement to stand in there and let her spew, there may be times when it is best to disengage until a better and more suitable time—especially when you feel your rage boiling up in retaliation.

Whatever the case, her rage is not an occasion for you to defend yourself. Her rage is hers and not an invitation for you to join the fray. It is our understanding that she must let it out, and that is something that you should not and cannot interfere with. Her rage may be best left to her to express among her women supporters—any one of whom can coach her better than you. (We do not suggest that you say that—that would be among the worst things you could do at the moment.) Rage for a woman is uniquely womanly and is best dealt with that way. Just like the anger/rage exercises we sometimes do in our men's circles, women know how to let each other vent, rage, and get it all out. But if it is here and now, your first job is to stand and take it—full on. Rage can be deadly to the relationship and to your valor if you are not capable of absorbing it and letting it happen. You must understand that you can suffer irreparable damage if you engage with her rage.

If one of your men were filled with rage against you, your men would make the two of you stand toe-to-toe and clean it up. You may walk away with a few bruises to your ego but the two of you would have vented your spleens and gotten it out, and more often than not, you would be even closer comrades than ever as a result. So you can do this—the only problem is that you must not retaliate, verbally or—and especially—physically.

The rule for dealing with her rage: DO NOT ENGAGE—DO NOT TALK—STAND THERE AND TAKE IT, THAT'S ALL! Once she has spewed all of her venom out at you and has stopped to catch her breath, the best thing for you to say is, "Thank you for telling me that; my gosh, I had no idea how badly I hurt you. I never intended to hurt you." (Use your own words, but you get the idea.) Try your best not to use qualifiers like "kind of" or "sort of"—just acknowledge that she is hurt and angry—Rage is always a protection for pain and anger. Again, you are well advised not to attempt to fix it—emotions do NOT need to be fixed and then, when she has calmed a bit, you might ask if there is anything she needs right then.

> *Survival Tip:* The moment you match your woman's rage with your own, you have lost. It is much harder to repair the damage when you have added to the destruction.

PUSHING YOUR BUTTONS

We all have sore spots in our personalities, chinks in our armor that when penetrated, cause us to lose our balance and lash out in defense. It could be a specific insecurity, like feeling that you're not as smart or as strong or as trustworthy as you want people to believe. Or a painful memory, like getting fired from a job (even if happened fifty years ago) can make someone sensitive to threats to job security or to perceived slights about his competence. These sore spots are commonly called buttons, and when your wife pushes yours, it's easy to stop listening and retaliate. Do you know what your buttons are—what hooks you into engaging in the "debate" even when you know better? Well, your woman knows. Having lived with your woman for x number of years, you can be sure that she has discovered all of your buttons, and is expert in pushing them at will. First, you might ask, "Why would she want to do this?"

C'mon, man, this is the classic shell game. If she can hook you into arguing when she is in a fighting mood then you become the culprit and she is off the hook for feeling that way. Button pushing can be offensive or defensive. She might not be sinister—it may just be a set of patterns the two of you have.

If you get to know your own buttons better than your wife does, you can begin to install that reset button to keep you balanced when your buttons get pushed. Working with your buttons is a three-step process: 1. Identify your buttons. 2. Start catching yourself when they get pushed. 3. Identify the cues coming directly before the reaction so that you can push the reset button in time.

<u>Identifying your buttons</u>

What are your insecurities? These are really your hottest buttons. If you are anything like us, there are things that your wife says that just set you off. These are usually issues around your trustworthiness and integrity (those are most men's main issues in life) or around her self-esteem[38] (most women's core issue—which she tries to get from you), but they can span a whole raft of topics. We would like to list a few examples of ours even though that might be a little too personal for a guide! What we have heard (in quotations) and the button thought that was triggered in us (in parenthesis).

"You are always criticizing me" (I need to have *some* opinions)

"It feels like you're going to leave" (I am committed to staying—forever)

"Fine—I'll just go get another boyfriend" (I had a partner who cheated on me before)

"I don't feel like I come first" (Ow, she doesn't, my purpose is first and kids are second—she is big and strong enough to fend for herself in an emergency)

"I don't trust you" (I have been untrustworthy in my past and try hardest on this)

---

38 Alison Armstrong says that one of the most painful things for the men she has interviewed is "how much women don't like themselves" when their men, in fact, adore them (p. 48).

In addition to these (add your own) buttons, your wife has internalized a list of your fuckups, shortcomings, and hurtful actions during the course of your life together, and she can use these to set you off ("I thought we buried that issue long ago!"). The longer you have been together, the bigger the list becomes.

Your buttons may not be apparent to you, because they feel like weaknesses, and we all tend to hide our weaknesses, even from ourselves. The sign that you have been set off by one of these buttons is if an argument or problem takes on greater emotional proportions than the situation warrants. Arguments and disagreements happen and there may be some anger or frustration associated with them, but too much intensity is a sure sign that somebody's button was pushed. If you have a good men's team that you have been a member of for some time or have a best buddy you've known for ages, they or he will be able to name all your buttons! Do your homework and get clear about the fact that you have them and they are YOUR buttons, despite the fact that she has learned how to push them.

By the way, your reaction might be just the opposite of lashing back. You may be someone who shuts down when the button gets hit. Brooding in your cave, hitting the heavy bag, or clenching your jaw so tightly your muscles hurt are hints that the jig is up—you have buttons.

Catching yourself

Catching yourself is not easy; mostly because it looks like she is doing something to you and therefore it looks like she has the problem. It looks like she keeps bringing the same things up over and over. WRONG! You have the button and anything that gets near it will set it off; your generalization of issues to those trigger topics is what is happening. The painful part of this process is that when you set out to catch yourself, you begin to realize how much more frequently you do it than you thought or were willing to admit.

Catching yourself requires figuring out some method of "spot-lighting" the moment. When I used to teach people how to stop biting their nails, I would give them a rubber band for their wrist. Each time they put their finger to their mouth, they were to give it a little snap—which would cause a short burst of awareness. If that works for you, try it, but if having a little notepad in your pocket or the console of the car works, do that. The first thing you might notice is that it looks like you are getting worse—but actually you are just getting more aware. Whatever you choose, once you start becoming conscious of your button moments, you need a capture mechanism. This is important: you need to capture both the button topic and what happened or was discussed just before it. These we call triggers, and the triggers are the real issue. Getting control of your triggers will disable the button.

Identifying the Triggers

Triggers are the thoughts, interpretations, and events that happen immediately before your button is pushed. Think of it this way—it is as simple as ABC. It is a technique called "cognitive re-structuring" borrowed from the psychologist Albert Ellis. He says dealing with this is a matter of ABC.

A. There's an **A**ction—your wife says something to you. This is an objective experience that's easy to write down when it happens.

B. You interpret it to mean something bad about you, because you have a **B**elief ("If she does that then she must think I am a schmuck."). This is a subjective, unconscious experience that takes some digging to become aware of and write down. When you look at them the Bs are your Buttons, and you are the one who brings them into play. In short, she doesn't really push your buttons—you do! She just says or does A.

C. As a Consequence, you react emotionally, and have a feeling, then you react physically, by walking away, or yelling back. This is another objective experience, but it's a little harder to be aware of and remember later so you can write it down.

A is the trigger—it's the triggering event. B is the button—the belief is the weakness. C is just a resulting consequence, a natural by-product of having engaged your buttons. Once you get this and do the required work of introspection to get at the entire array of buttons you sport on your control panel, you can begin to take control of things. But it is a process of working backward from the consequences.

This is something you can dig through with your men, and it takes some working on to get it. So keep at it and find your Trigger beliefs. By the way, in keeping with the "simple as ABC" theme, we would add a fourth part in getting control of your triggers—"D." Dealing with your belief triggers means "disputing" the logic (or illogic) of a belief.

D. You need to Dispute that what she has said or done "means" that you are or have been wrong—or that it "means" anything at all. By interrupting the chain reaction of your belief system ("if she thinks this then I must be that"), you can become an observer and listener to what your wife is actually saying. She may just be giving you a report on the state of her internal being; she may be telling you what she needs or that you have totally missed the mark on something.

By not engaging the belief button, you have a better shot of hearing that and acting appropriately. D is a kind of "reset" button. Are there other possible interpretations? Could she be meaning something else by what she said or did?

<u>Should I stay or should I go?</u>

Sometimes in a heated argument, it feels like the lyrics from a song from The Clash: "If I go there will be trouble, if I stay it will be double." Fortunately, Kenny Rogers has some advice: "You gotta know when to hold 'em, know when to fold 'em." As we have said, it's important to hang in there when your wife is upset with you and listen as much as you possibly can. But it's even more important not to get drawn into a heated argument. So when she's "pushed one of your buttons," you have a split second to make the right decision. If you've done the work to identify your triggers and buttons and knock back the false beliefs, you might be able to hang in there and listen to your wife. But if you feel yourself spinning out of control, at least the awareness that your button has been pushed will allow you to disengage temporarily until you regain your composure. Huffing or slinking away with your tail tucked is not going to help, nor is just walking away without an explanation. You need to say something like, "You know what, I think I am getting really cranked and I recognize that I am doing this discussion no good, so please give me a few minutes (substitute your own time frame here) and then let's come back to it." Plus, this requires discussing that tactic with your wife ahead of time. In calmer times let her know that you are working on this and that you need a way not to make issues bigger than they are. You do not need to name your buttons; you do not have to reveal any dark secrets. You just have to talk about the need to be cleaner and fairer in disagreements and that you recognize you have a tendency to make bigger issues out of some things. It helps to agree on a code word or phrase that will let you (or her) break off or take a time out.

One last point here: you play the game just as much as she does. Over time, you have learned what her buttons are and you know when and how to push them. Don't play innocent—fess up! Now get to work on the same three steps so you can catch yourself pushing *her* buttons, then cut it out. You are not serving anyone playing this petty little game!

> **Survival Tip:** With your men's team, spend time identifying each other's hooks and buttons. Work backward to find your triggers and begin monitoring them.

WINNING BACK HER TRUST

O K, so you blew it. We all do at one time or another. The question you are facing is: if your screwup has significantly damaged your credibility and thus her trust in you as her protector and partner in life, then how might you find your way back to her favor? First the bad news: you might not ever get back to the same level you may once have had. That's just the long and short of it. Many women have a hard time forgiving, especially when what her man did threatened her sense of safety and security. As we have said before, most women have self-esteem issues and nearly all of them live with some level of fear or concern for their safety (the "prey" syndrome). So if the bomb of what you did exploded near either of those, you may have a long uphill journey with a rather large boulder to push!

Moreover, women tend to retain a detailed memory of things you have done that have caused pain or threatened their sense of safety, and these are their reference points when things degenerate seriously. When they perceive the balance of power to be tilted against them and the fear of being hurt or overpowered becomes imminent, out comes the reference file, "This just like the time when you..." If the current hurt is big or serious, out will come the big, bad serious ones of the past. Some of your more egregious errors and screwups will be at the head of that list if she feels really threatened. (By the way, she likely does not refer to this as some kind of intentional list or even something "intentional" at all. It is more something that we men perceive than something that they are intentionally doing.) So you can tell how big your current fuckup is by the nature and size of the list items she compares it to. Damage done—retreat, regroup your thoughts, and move into Plan B—winning back her trust.

There are two things to consider in winning back your woman's trust once she has gone into that protective recoil. One is that we must consider the nature of trust and how and what constitutes trust and being trustworthy—worthy of her trust. Secondly, and, in our minds, more importantly, trust goes hand in hand with integrity, and since integrity is the more important and more difficult of the two buddies, let's start there.

Integrity refers to the match between the outside and inside—between the things you do (outside) and the reasons you do them (inside). Matching your actions and your intentions is tricky. Many men think that what they are doing is a perfect readout of their finest intentions, but those around them may smell something else. How many times have you heard a man say something like, "Look, you can count on me for that," and just know in your guts that it won't happen? That is because you are actually picking up something out of kilter. When he fails to deliver, the man is "out of integrity," as we are calling it. The words and the music just don't match! Yet he may have sworn on a stack of Bibles that he was good for his promise. He sees only his intention and all he knows is what he "thinks" is true for him.

Now without getting into the psychology of the why and how of it, let's just assume the above to be a fairly commonplace occurrence—that you notice the gap between what a man says and what you perceive is the truth. How can he or anyone bridge that integrity gap? If that man is you, the first thing you need to know is that you cannot do it by yourself—it is kind of like trying to see the back of your head. But the issue with integrity is that you can see only what you intend to be doing and thus, you will never be able to see that what you are actually doing is not in sync with what you intended. Furthermore, you will not be "out of integrity" most of the time. Generally we are all working to show up as the man we think we are and that produces a good deal of alignment—most of the time. But when you're off, you will need a good group of trusted men to help you, and it will take loads of practice. Here's an exercise we call the "I am" exercise that will start moving you in the right direction.

Start off by completing the sentence, "I am…" Think, for example, of the Boy Scout code—"trustworthy, loyal, kind, etc." You might say, "I am committed to being the greatest husband a wife could ever want." It really doesn't matter what you say, so long as it is something you mean and really believe to be true about yourself, but it should be short and to the point. Once you are clear on your "I am" sentence, stand up in front of your men's team and say it to them. Then ask: "Feedback?" Your team of listeners should have been instructed and prepared to give you feedback—a thumbs-up or thumbs-down. Thumbs-up means that what the man heard and how you said it were in perfect harmony—that he sensed that you were in integrity with yourself. Thumbs-down means that there was something out of whack with the how and why of your sentence. Each man will hear different things and some may even hear you as being in integrity when others don't. What you are looking for eventually is all thumbs-up!

So, turning to each man who gives you thumbs-down, you ask, "What was off for you?" Your men should be instructed to give their feedback (individually) like this: "I heard what you said, but it sounds like..." The end of the sentence could be anything they perceive ranging from "you don't believe it yourself" to "you aren't telling the whole story" or even, "something is missing—I don't know, but I just don't get it!" An alternative response from your men can be, "What was missing for me in what you said was..." But either way, it is important that the men follow this pattern of speaking and that they don't just say something like, "Well, that sucked!" By structuring their responses in this way, you can get specific information on where your speaking and acting are out of integrity. But don't have the men correct your grammar or tell you what you should say—just what they heard as missing or out of integrity about what you said.

Once you get your feedback from each "thumbs-down" man, take it in and try your "I am" sentence again, asking for feedback once again after you say it. By the way, you will immediately notice that you get more thumbs-down the second time than the first time, simply because you are trying too hard and are disingenuous in your speaking—that is really what being out of integrity looks and feels like! So suck it up, take in the feedback, and try your sentence again, and again, until you get all thumbs-up. *And something very powerful will happen at that point.* When you finally do get it, you won't even have to ask for feedback. The men will just spontaneously give you the unanimous thumbs-up! When that happens, stop in your tracks and take a full-body readout. How are you feeling? How are you standing? Where is your center? Get a clear picture of what being in integrity—for just that one sentence—feels, acts, and looks like. By the way, we have actually videotaped this exercise and you can see a visible difference between the first and last state the man was in—it is that noticeable. So get this straight: being in integrity is more than just not bullshitting your wife. It is an actual physical, emotional, and cognitive state change that is both hard to accomplish and even more difficult to maintain. *Being in integrity will take practice.*

Now let's turn to trust. What is it that we humans actually trust? Do you trust that the sun will come up? Of course! Because every day, without fail, it comes up. We trust that when we turn the faucet with the H on it, hot water will come out—and most of the time it does. So the core of creating trust is consistency over an extended set of actions and situations. Trust is not built on one action. In fact, once trust has been violated (the net result of your having hurt her), your good actions appear only to be an exception. The general rule here is that trust is kind of like the thirty-day moving average on the stock market (if REA is the stock, then trust is the moving average). It lags behind and takes several weeks of wins to have it trail up and come close to actual performance because each uptick is averaged in with all of the performance over the past thirty days. In the case of your wife's distrust, this might well be a ninety-day moving average, or more! Trust is just that hard to win. However, once it is there, the moving average still works—like when the boiler breaks and hot water doesn't come out, we don't lose trust in the H, we fix the boiler and go on trusting.

Integrity and trust have to work together. You must be acting in integrity—doing the right things for the right reasons—and you have to do that consistently over an extended period. When your integrity is high and your consistency is solid, you can slip every once in a while without sustaining too much damage. Your integrity and trust are your lifeline—like the belay rope a climber has on a cliff. If you slip, your integrity rope will catch you. You might get a skinned knee, and you have to scramble to get back to where you were, but integrity keeps you up there and you haven't fallen to your death. That's what can happen when you don't have your integrity!

Survival Tip: What you say doesn't matter—it's what you do and continue to do consistently that will make the difference. Focus on your commitment and you will remain consistent.

FORGIVING

"The weak can never forgive. Forgiveness is the attribute of the strong."
Mahatma Gandhi

"A woman will forgive a man anything, except his failure
to ask to be forgiven."
Rumi

Now, let's turn the tables. Your woman will invariably do something at one time or another that will just plain piss you off. That is to be expected when two people of different makeups, from different families and backgrounds live together. There are bound to be differences—in agendas, in values, and in needs. Expect that and you will not have nearly as many problems to start with. But that will not preclude the possibility of her really getting your goat.

So what are you to do? The simple man-answer is, "Get over it!" But what that translates to is forgiving her. That is your task and perhaps your number one challenge. Several times throughout this guide, we have referred to your need to lose the right/wrong distinction. That's easy to say, but what does it really mean to forgive one's lover, one's spouse, one's life partner? How do you actually go about doing that?

Start by recognizing what game you are playing. If you are playing the little petty game of who's right and who's wrong, you will inevitably lose the big game of committed marriage for life. Remember, it may sometimes be better to lose the battle and live to fight another day, and perhaps to win the war, than to go all out and win this one at the expense of everything. What will you win anyway, if you win this skirmish? A trophy? A medal? Some stripe on your epaulet?

It does not have to look good. Have you ever ridden a bucking bronco? The name of that game is stay in the saddle for seven seconds—no matter what it looks like! Staying in the marriage is at times like riding a really wild steed, and your job is to stay in the saddle. Does the cowboy care whether his bronco circles left or right? Does he even know which way it is going to go next? Hell, no! His focus is to keep his balance and his wits about him and stay in the damned saddle. We saw one contest where it was apparent that the cowboy had pissed his pants—but he stayed on and that was all that counted.

How strong are you, anyway? Any weakling can get pissed and cop an attitude, but it takes a huge man and a truckload of strength to forgive. How tough are you? Where do you have to go inside yourself and what is the conversation you need to have with your ego in order to forgive? Remember, the full phrase is to forgive *and* forget! Not only do you need to let go of this thing she did or said, without any potential for reward, but you also have to bury it and forget it ever happened. That takes strength of character. Our challenge to you is to push yourself to be that kind of man, that strong in character and commitment to your marriage.

Forgiving is "fore—giving," that is, granting her the grace to give back that state that you had be-*fore* this battle began. Can you recall how you loved her before? Can you recall some part of her that constantly delighted you then? Can you conjure up an image of her eyes as she looked at you in adoration? That is the "fore" of forgiving. Try to hold that picture of her and reset your imaging of her to that scene and you will literally be giving back that state from before. It is like hitting the reset button on your computer! Simply "tolerating" this error of hers will only lead to greater resentment. It must be thoroughly obliterated from your memory. *Reset!*

So, then, what do you do at that point? If you have "fore-given" and have remembered that woman, that look, that state from before, remember what you would have done at that point or in that state. How powerfully transforming would it be—in the middle of a fight—to suddenly shift and, remembering that this is your woman of choice, suddenly hug her and say something like, "I don't want to argue anymore, I just remembered how much I really love you. That's more important. It is OK if we do what you want!" Of course she may still be angry with you or ranting or crying, but not only does your *non sequitur* have the potential to interrupt her pattern, it also ices in the fore-giving for you and helps you to return to where you need to be. The only caution here is that you must be certain that you are coming from integrity—that you, in truth, have already forgiven and forgotten. At the very least, the break in the action will give you the space to say that you both might want some time to regroup your thoughts, and then give her some time and space by breaking off.

Now if the problem is that she cheated on you, that is symptomatic of a bigger problem and you need to go to the next section.

Survival Tip: Practice letting go—it is called forgiving and forgetting. Let her hold all the resentments and "hurt memories" she wants but that is not a masculine trait. Learn what you need to do to let it go.

SECTION 6

MEDICAL EMERGENCIES

"Plane crashes rarely happen in real life the same way they happen in the movies. Some engine part does not explode in a fiery bang. The rudder doesn't suddenly snap under the force of takeoff. The captain doesn't gasp, 'Dear God,' as he is thrown back against his seat. The typical commercial jetliner—at this point in its stage of development—is about as dependable as a toaster. Plane crashes are more likely to be the result of an accumulation of minor difficulties and seemingly trivial malfunctions."

Malcolm Gladwell

Whether it's a snakebite or a broken bone, medical emergencies alter the trip. It is no longer about exploring or "getting there," your focus is now on surviving. Break-ups, affairs, separation, and divorce have a similar effect on the path of marriage—now damage control and reparation take center stage.

(Kris and Dave)

THE UH-OH CHAPTER (DIVORCE AND SEPARATION)

So this is the chapter that is definitely not fun to read, especially if this is actually happening. As we said at the opening, this guide may piss you off; well, this chapter is the bad news that will push you over the edge—because we will not tolerate anything less than full ownership of the whole problem—your ownership.

So it comes down to this: she wants out—the marriage is dry—you suck and what's more you always have. The litany starts something like that, and the bottom line is that the marriage has fallen on the rocks and you didn't even see it coming. Hey, you were going along minding your own business, being the breadwinner, keeping the cars tuned and safe—whatever. And suddenly your wife says that she is bored, hurt, neglected...and pissed!

And from what you glean from her tirade, you are to blame. Maybe she has already closed you off and is talking to the lawyer or, worse yet, having an affair.

What you need to get into your head from the outset is that this is not a repair job that has a quick fix. You are in deep shit and you do not have even a shovel to begin the task of getting out of the smell. What's more, you need to look squarely at how you have been the cause of the problem. This is the big league; this is the NFL and these are bone-crushing hits you are getting. It took some time to make this happen and it will take a lot more to undo it. The emotion that a woman feels when she says the "D" word is the most powerful emotion a woman can possess. Most often, it is just like Rage (review the section on a Woman's Rage). Generally speaking, women in relationships want to be caring and supportive. So when her nature has turned to this extreme, the intensity she must muster to come out with her full anger intensifies the anger into a full rage. This intense emotion is an arrow that can penetrate your thick and shiny armor, bring you to your knees, and have you bleed to a certain death. Most men don't see it coming, and when this arrow hits, they want to immediately pull it out. I want you to imagine for the rest of this chapter, that you can't pull it out. It has penetrated your heart, and if you pull it out you will bleed to death instantly. Your only hope is to break it off at the surface of your chest, and have your body heal around it. But there is hope.

In co-ed workshops, we have often asked women, "What can we do to regain your trust once we have violated it?" What we find interesting is that most women are dumbfounded and come up short of any kind of satisfactory answer. They just can't answer the question. Why? Because first and foremost, women act from their feeling state. As John Gray often says, how they feel more often than not determines how they will react, and in the depth of hurt, that is all they can see and feel. In other words, asking her what is wrong will get you either the killer "nothing!" or everything. Either way it will be of no help to you in determining what to do and how to repair the damage. This is something you will have to do, and most likely, <u>you</u> will have to do it without her cooperation.

So you have to start off by getting clear about yourself. What do you want? Do you want this relationship or not? Let's take a wild-ass guess at what you want. It is the same five (to pick an arbitrary number) things for mostly all men.

You want shelter. You're bright enough (we hope) to get out of the rain and into your home to not get wet. Most of us, however, have probably thought that a cave would be a great place to live if we were not so domesticated.

You want food and drink. A necessity for sure, but still a want. You know the facts that you cannot survive for long without food and water, so they make it begrudgingly onto the list.

You want sex. In a perfect world, you would get it when you wanted and how you wanted it. But like most men you somehow equate sex with sustenance, acceptance, and health (often in that order—most of us being convinced that on our deathbed we could still get it up).

And you want success. You want to be good at something that earns you acknowledgement, respect, power, and privilege. *But you don't need to be married to have any of those five things.* And when you have entered a relationship to obtain them, you have set up a dynamic that can cause great damage—not to you or her, but to the relationship.

The relationship is not you, not her, or you and her. Think of the relationship as third person, which we shall call "R" for reference, and because we don't like typing so much! R is like another person that resides with the two of you, day in and day out. There are a few things you need to know about R. Your job is to fuel R with all your gifts. Many of these gifts are in this guide. Listening, loving, patience, and being spontaneous, are just a few. When you don't give R sustenance, you will create the situation you are in now. Let's say it again. Your job is to constantly, every possible moment of every day and night, fuel R with everything you have. Now, here is the secret. Your wife will take what you have given to R and do what she wants with it. Your wife is the only person who will decide if R lives or dies. You have no control over that. Your job is to give to it unconditionally. And when you don't you can cause severe harm.

When divorce is imminent it may seem sometimes that R is terminal with some disease, and it seems hopeless or a waste of time to fuel her. You may do something nice for the relationship, and it will immediately disintegrate. (Dave's story about bringing home flowers for his wife is a great example.) DON'T BE DISIL-LUSIONED! You must be relentless and never give up on giving it all of your gifts. Don't ever try to figure out what R needs. Just keep giving, supporting, loving her, and let your wife decide what to do with it. This is the sole reason why "50/50" relationships fail. You have no clue about how to manage R. She does. You don't possess the feminine qualities and emotional skills for nurturing a relation-ship and what it takes to keep it working and successful. She does. So, if she handles 50 percent of the relationship, and you man-handle the other 50 percent, then you are being counterproductive and the relationship has only half a chance of surviving. Your job is to give to it unconditionally—100 percent—and let her decide if R is having a good or bad day. One last time. Your wife will decide if R will live or die; you don't possess the skills to sustain its life or prevent its death.

What is your commitment? Now don't be a woman and act from your feelings here! You gave your word when you committed to marry her that you would not abandon her. And over the years she has, by lack of adoration, fallen into disrepair. Maybe she is fat or dumpy, maybe she doesn't do her hair anymore or wears it in some masculine-looking buzz cut (sorry about the slur), maybe she wears sweats all day long and you haven't seen her

> When I got married, I said for better or worse. Well, come to find out, "worse" includes a whole ton of shit that I don't like. AND—I'm staying right here.

thighs in years. Who cares? That does not matter. Did you ever take a look at a rosebush that you haven't cared for in years? It is just a bramble with too many thorns and little flowers. And what happens when you don't change the oil in your car or wash the winter salt off? Your woman is just like that rosebush or the car that you drive. If you spent time taking care of her as you do your car you are guaranteed much better results. Little wonder that the relationship has fallen into disrepair.

What is your commitment? If you have kids, then you have no choice. You have a responsibility to them to provide fatherly parenting. And the simple truth is that there are only a couple of states in the Union that have any semblance of father's rights in divorce. In one neighboring state, there is *not one single case on record* of a father winning custody in the *history* of that state (last time we checked, which admittedly was back in 2003 or so). If you divorce, not only do you lose, your children lose more. Kids need fathering and the greatest abuse that people report from childhood is an absent father—more so than an abusing father! You leave and you are committing child abuse! It is as simple as that. (We will say more about this in the next section.)

What is your commitment? What did you commit to your wife? Why did you marry her? You need to dig deep and dig fast because that is the rock you have to anchor your work on. Do you want to be just another statistic of American divorce? This is not OK with us, but you are a man, do what you will, and if you just can't muster the gumption to get back in there and fight then we simply ask that you give this book to someone who can use it and go lick your self-important wounds elsewhere!

One of the fundamental truths about becoming a man is learning that your life is not about you. Unless you have a purpose greater than yourself, your life as a man will be self-absorbed and petty. Ask yourself if you have a purpose—and are you on purpose.

Consider the following...

Imagine coming home one day and finding your wife in bed with another man.

If your reaction is "No big deal," then close this book and give it to someone else.

If your reaction is any of the thousand feelings like remorse, rage, envy, exasperation, etc., then you do care and there is hope. You will have a reaction only if you really care and, if that is the case, then it makes sense to do all you can to win her back.

Read on.

First things first: Your commitment determines your actions and your feelings—not her. If you are *just* committed to making it work, you're doomed. Your commitment needs to be way bigger than making it work. Your commitment, your stand for the marriage has to be greater than anything else you have ever done in your life—it has to be as big as your life purpose. That means that each day, each hour, each action has to be driven by your purposeful commitment—*not* by what is happening in the marriage. So get committed.

Now you have to face the first test of your new resolve. We mentioned this in passing before, but allow us to drive it in a little further. As we mentioned early on, the equal and opposite reaction shows up all over the place and here is no exception. Just because you decided to make a turnaround does not mean she will get weak in the knees! In fact, the "equal and opposite" will most probably occur. That means that the stronger you want her and want this to work out, the more likely it is that she will meet that with an equal level of repulsion. In fact, we encourage you to look at her equal and opposite reaction as a confirmation that you made a strong commitment. The harder her rejection of your initial work, the more likely you are showing up to the universe as committed. (We know this sounds backward, but that is the nature of things—the universal laws are not human laws and are most often counterintuitive, or the dead opposite of our human logic!) You have to understand that even your actions will not prove anything to her, at least in the beginning. Her emotions will not let her believe that you are committed to the relationship, and you will be met with more negative emotions like rejection, disgust, anger, disappointment, and contempt. You must be relentless in your pursuit and your commitment—that is the first step.

Secondly, recall what you did to win her in the first place. It is unlikely that you won her over on the first date or with that first roll in the hay! Most of us, in order to get a yes vote on the marriage ballot, had to court our future spouses. Courting has two main functions: One, it was totally other-serving. You did not do things for you, you did them all for her—where you went, what you ate, the treats you savored—all to please her. This is not selling out, but an extreme focusing on her needs and desires. The act of focusing on her increased your attention to a level of infatuation with her. You "fell in love" with her scent, her eye color, her silly laugh, whatever! In truth, you most likely didn't have what we would call a mature love but rather an infatuation. And it was totally a function of the second aspect of courtship: the intensity of your focus.

A few years ago Kris' wife was coming up on a significant birthday, so he wanted to make it a sensational party. He took a whole year planning this event, involving a team of women and friends to make it happen. And there was not a day in that year that he did not do at least one thing or at least have a call with the team focusing on his wife. The net result wasn't so much that he created a super party—the net result was that about three-quarters of the way through the year, he had fallen so in love with this woman all over again! And he still is! Now, that wasn't a damaged relationship, but it does show the point for our side of the equation—focus exclusively on her and your infatuation factor will increase.

In order to win her back, you have to get back to that core. This is a monumental feat. Not very many men have the support and willpower to take this feat on with enough power to win. Every man has the power to make a difference. But remember, your wife has 100 percent control over whether the relationship lives or dies. Not you. Your job is to fuel R with everything you have, and be relentless in that pursuit—to focus on your wife and become totally other-serving.

What is the measure of your success? Well, if R lives, then that is success. There are probably many other ways to measure success. What you really need to do is check in with yourself every day, multiple times a day, or have a man in your life check in with you to ask you if you are bringing your BEST to the relationship. If you believe that you are, and you are inspected by other men that conclude you are, then that is all you can do.

Survival Tip: Have you fallen out of focus (and thus out of enchantment) with your wife? Focus on her daily—do at least one thing each day exclusively about her and watch the magic reappear.

Relationships in Separation...

So things haven't gone exactly the way you would have wanted them to and you have (or she has) moved out. There are two conditions we need to consider here: either you have kids or you don't. If you don't have kids and you are committed to being married to this woman you have chosen, then go back to the beginning of this guide and commit it to memory. Likewise, if you have no kids, and frankly are done with the relationship—have a nice life, but before you ever venture down this path again, reread the guide and practice these principles in all your dating and courtship. It could serve you in the next marriage.

...with kids in the picture.

But if you have kids the picture changes. Your first priority is to be a dad. It is because of you that they were conceived in the first place. You own that responsibility and you need to step up to the responsibility. There is no discussion needed here—get past the fact that she is at fault or you are at fault or whatever you have made up about your circumstances. The fact—pure and simple—is that you are a dad first, a husband and all else after that.

Kids need dads. Parenting takes both mothering and fathering—and those are completely different processes. Not only is it unfair to expect their mother to be both father and mother, it is illogical. A mother cannot and should not try to be a dad. The father role is specific and special to kids. You show your boys what a man of honor is and how to be a stand for something in this world of wimps and weasels! (Sorry—did we really say that?) You also show your girls the type of man that is out there for them to choose as a mate—one who is valiant and value driven. Would you want anything less for your girls? Of course not! You need to and must stay closely involved in their lives.

And perhaps one of the biggest aspects of the father role is that of supporting the mother in doing her job—not as substitute moms, or in keeping an accounting of the number of hours each has spent caring for the kids. Supporting the mother, according to Kyle and Marsha Pruett, means joint emotional ownership and creating a sense of teamwork that children experience as solid.[39]

Let us drive home the point here with some staggering stats:
Children from fatherless homes account for:[40]

- 63 percent of youth suicides. (Source: US Dept. of Health & Human Services, Bureau of the Census).
- 71 percent of pregnant teenagers. (Source: US Dept. of Health & Human Services)
- 90 percent of all homeless and runaway children.
- 70 percent of juveniles in state-operated institutions come from fatherless homes. (Source: U.S. Dept. of Justice, Special Report, Sept. 1988)

---

39 Pruett, pp. 36-41

40 Courtesy of Children's Justice on line source at http://www.childrensjustice.org/stats.htm

- 85 percent of all children that exhibit behavioral disorders. (Source: Center for Disease Control).
- 80 percent of rapists motivated with displaced anger. (Source: Criminal Justice & Behavior, Vol. 14, pp. 403-26, 1978).
- 71 percent of all high school dropouts. (Source: National Principals Association Report on the State of High Schools).
- 75 percent of all adolescent patients in chemical abuse centers. (Source: Rainbows for all God's Children).
- 85 percent of all youths sitting in prisons. (Source: Fulton Co. Georgia jail populations, Texas Dept. of Corrections 1992).

And all of that damage is the result of having an absent father. Is that what you want? We thought not!

How you relate to your kids is extremely important.[41] First, do not miss a single school or extracurricular event. Even if you may have been in the habit of letting Mom do all that when you two were together, the time has come to step it up a notch or three. Get their calendar and talk it over with your wife. Make sure that she knows that you intend to be there to support your and her kids too. If the two of you are cut off (actually, if she has cut off communications with you) and not in regular communication, then get the information from the kids.

Most importantly, never, never, never bad-mouth your wife in front of the kids. That is what you have a men's team for. Go there and bitch and moan all you want or need—get it out of your system, and get over it. But with your kids, praise her. Even if they

---

41 (And here we are assuming that the kid(s) are living with their mom, your estranged wife in that, since the latter part of the twentieth century, mothers have been awarded primary custody in close to 90 percent of the court cases in the United States and, as we stated, in one Northeast state, 100 percent of the cases over the last fifty years.)

complain (and kids will complain—in fact if they discover that you two are on the outs with each other, they will actually try to play one against the other), you must take the high road and correct them. Tell them that their mom is the greatest and that perhaps she is stressed or hurting but she deserves your praise, love, and support and theirs as well. Make up games and ideas that the kids and you can do for her. And don't quit.

Now you are not doing it for this reason (because it is a father's job), but the other thing you should know is that she will judge you mostly (perhaps even exclusively now that she doesn't see you in any other realm) on the basis of how you treat her kids. Whatever your disagreements, whatever you feel about her, you need to dispense with that before you are around the kids. Kids are a hell of a lot smarter and intuitive than most adults give them credit for. They will pick up on the slightest insincerity that you may harbor—so be clean, and get to a point where you are sincere and genuine in your support of her and the kids.

Other things you can do include calling her up and offering her an extra night off, saying that you'll stop off and get takeout and take care of the kids tonight. Or if she is not that spontaneous, plan a little ahead for next week. You may have had to agree to be living separately but that does not relieve you of your commitment and duty. Exceed her expectations, and exceed your required duties.

But—and we want to make this perfectly clear—you do not have the luxury or even the choice of *not* fulfilling your responsibility. In fact, you have no other option than to work your level best to get the relationship back together and to get back in the house with your kids. There is no other option—no ifs, ands, or buts. Period. End of story. Get over it and get back in there! OK?

... AND IN DIVORCE

In the event that your efforts are too little or too late and a divorce has already been executed, you still have a relationship that you are in with your ex-wife (that is, when there are kids involved). The relationship with your ex is almost exclusively around the kids and their activities, but it is a relationship nonetheless. Most importantly, your support of the kids must include the support of their mom—and we mean more than just the child support payments! You have a primary job to make the life of your kids as "normal" as possible despite the divorce. Divorce is the most prevalent psychologically confusing, upsetting, and disruptive event in a child's life—to the point where we are tempted to refer to it as abuse.

The most confusing thing to kids is that somehow they figure that people get married in love and that they were conceived as a part or by-product of that love. Therefore, in their calculating little childlike brains, they figure that if you two do not love each other anymore, then they too are damaged at the very source of their being (you two). You both must be clear in communicating to them that your problems: 1) are not their problems, 2) are not of their doing or fault, and 3) in no way alter or change the love in which they were conceived. You will have to drill that message in over many years until your kids tell you to stop—that they get it. Until then do not stop.

Here are a few other things you could do. Never stop praising her (we don't care how much of a bitch she was, is, or can be) if you have kids. Send her Mother's Day cards, send her gifts, and always send her unprompted praise for her work as the mother of your children. If she is dating or remarried, support her relationship with him and his relationship with your kids. Send them a gift card for a dinner out and make the time to take your kids so that they can go out. Let us be clear, this is not rolling over to play doormat. You do this to support your kids, and to create sanity in their lives.

(A brief tale from Kris) I got divorced from my previous wife with whom I had two kids. I had made a lot of really stupid choices that cost me the marriage, and warranted her wrath. But when I discovered that the depression I felt was a direct result of how committed I was to my kids, I made up my mind to be the best father in divorce that there ever was. This was despite the certainty that my ex felt that I would disappear just like the bastard she had as a father had done. After several years of doing the above and going to school events (driving two hundred miles round-trip on a weeknight after work sometimes) and going to countless dance recitals, we were sitting beside each other at a dance competition our girls were in, and were approached by another couple. "We wanted to thank you guys," the man said. "You see, we're divorced and we used to come on alternating years. But we heard that you guys were divorced and we saw how you were both here cheering for your girls, and, well, that's what we do now. Thanks for being such a great model!"

Never give up—you never know how big of a change you can make.

Survival Tip: No matter what happens, you are still the father to your kids. If kids are involved you must stay focused on being the best you can for them. No kids means less difficulty, but still you must always take the higher path.

HAVING AN AFFAIR

*"No matter how happily a woman may be married, it always pleases her
to discover that there is a nice man who wishes that she were not."*

H. L. Mencken

Don't—don't go there! Period. End of sentence. Good-bye.
'Nuff said.

Look, we understand that at times the woman you
live with and have committed to sharing your life with, to growing old with, yeah her, *that* woman, can be a (check the appropriate
bullet below):

o   Royal pain in the ass
o   Bitch
o   Holy horror
o   Major problem

But she is your pain/bitch/horror/problem. Furthermore, we
recognize that the source of her being that way might not necessarily be you. So what? Deal with it. That is what marriage is all

about—dealing with the issues. Hey, any fool can deal with the ideal woman who is never a problem. It doesn't take skill to do that! But when she is too much to take, hanging in there takes real skill.

And having an affair because she has shut you out, or because she has become more problematic than you want to deal with, or because some young thing has winked at you will not only make matters worse, it will result in your now having two problems not one. So to start this section, let's lay down some basic rules concerning having an affair:

Rule #1—It is not a matter of *IF* she will ever find out, it is only a matter of *WHEN* she will find out![42*] One of the basic differences between men and women is that men tend to show loyalty by withholding and protecting state secrets. We know we can trust a man when he repeatedly demonstrates that he is worthy of confidentiality by not talking to others about what happened. Women, on the other hand, establish trusting circles by sharing secrets. It is their way of including another at the most intimate and trusting level. (Remember the "stain" on Monica Lewinski's dress? How do you think that story got out?) So, this being the case, that doe-eyed "understanding" woman you might consider spilling your guts with, and your seed in, will *need* to share her secret with others. It is only a matter of time until her circles of influence cross paths with your wife's. So from the very beginning you better be aware of the fact—and it is a raw, cold, hard fact—that she *will* find out. At that point, you just might as well move on to the divorce chapter, because philandering is ample grounds for divorce in any state.

Rule #2—Comparisons kill! There is a law in optics called the "Mach band." It refers to the illusion of contrast when, say, a

---

42* Credit goes again to our buddy Rich O'Keeffe for this maxim.

sheet of white paper is next to a sheet of dark gray or black paper. Right at the edge, the contrast is heightened making the white look brighter and the gray or black look even darker black. Diverting your attention to any other woman than your wife will produce the same effect. Not only will the contrast seem heightened, but it will be generalized to the entire sheet of paper, which in this case is both your wife and your potential mistress. Those behaviors that were formerly only ancillary irritants (i.e., not the big problems) will take on heightened proportions and make her downright ugly. Your irritation will grow into anger and disgust. Every aspect of her; her breathing, her hygiene, her voice, her perfume, everything will become more irritating in contrast to this warm seductive body with whom you are now entertaining the notion of an affair. By contrast, the other woman will take on superlative qualities. She will suddenly develop runway model characteristics. She will become more radiant, more voluptuous, and more irresistible than you ever imagined. And you will suddenly be unable to control your inner desires.

Don't be a fool—it is just the optics of the Mach band!

Rule #3—The Groucho Marx Club. Groucho was once quoted as saying that he "would not want to be a member of any club that would have [him] as a member." Applied to the affair situation—now you have to follow this convoluted logic here—you are talking to a woman who: 1) knows you are married; 2) thinks that she might be able to seduce you away, and then subsequently; 3a) believes that you will never be unfaithful to her, so long as ye both shall live; or 3b) thinks that you are worthy of her love, having just been a philandering son-of-a-bitch to your wife! Does that strike you as logical and rational? If it does, we have some names of therapists in your area you may want to consult (actually any one will do!).

So the bottom line here is that affairs, though practiced since the beginning of time, are not all they are cracked up to be and certainly not worth the pain that they eventually cause. Our solution is simple:

Have an affair with your wife. (Yeah, her)

Look—your wanting to have an affair is not about your wife. (Here is another one of those things we are going to shove in your face that you will not like.) It is all about you. From all we can tell (having talked to bunches of men over the years), it comes from one of two sources: either your desire is your infantile and immature ego trying to feel good about itself because you haven't developed the balls to stand on your own and take the licks being dished out—so your childish ego wants to run away and hide—or it is a spiritual quest (or the yearning for a spiritual quest) that is misdirected.[43]

Let's assume for the moment that you don't want to admit the former, so we'll talk about the quest. As men, one of the most spiritual moments we experience is sexual intimacy and orgasm. At that moment we feel invincible and yet totally open to the world. Our senses are heightened and we feel fully alive and alert. We yearn to be that way—always—who wouldn't want to be invincible and on top of the world? But it isn't sex that does it—that is just where we feel it perhaps for the first time. As maturing men, we must go on deeper and deeper quests to advance our understanding of ourselves. Each of those quests and the pain associated with them will chip away at our egos, strengthening and maturing us. But misdirecting that toward philandering or sleeping about will inevitably prove to be empty. Our recommendation is to check out some of

---

43 Robert Moore and Douglas Gillette, "Initiation and the Male Spiritual Quest," in *Redeeming Men: Religion and Masculinities*, Stephen Boyd, et al., eds., Westminster John Knox Press, Louisville, KY, 1996, pp.187-196.

the men's initiation rituals and weekends at the back of this guide. You are sure to find some de-layering happening there.

As for the former issue—you need to wake up and recognize that it is just such pain that will mature you. Your wife is actually doing you a huge favor by what she is doing—whether she knows it or not—and the associated discomfort you experience, will be the catalyst that will help you grow and mature. If you get the right guidance through this passage, you have the potential to become much larger and certainly more mature as a result. But to do that means that parts of your ego must die—not you, just your childish, immature, self-centered ego. What doesn't kill you will make you better. But maybe you don't appreciate such theoretical talk so let's use an example of what this might "look like" in real life.

First, let's lay down some ridiculous (or not so ridiculous) assumptions—we'll call it the worst-case scenario (WCS). You are both getting on in age and maybe you (she bore them) have had a couple of kids and so her body is not the one you fell in love with. Her breasts are sagging, maybe her muscles are flabby, and her vagina is no longer tight and juicy, like it once was. She is tired all the time and has been complaining of having the longest lasting case of post-partum depression in the annals of the *New England Journal of Medicine!* By contrast (for the WCS), you are the picture of health, a gracefully aging GQ model with just the right touch of gray at the temples and not even your Polo shirt can hide that swarthy fit'n'trim body you sport underneath! In the WCS you, sir, are a stud!

Anything less than the WCS above we will consider infinitely closer and easier to accomplish—fair enough? Now what you are faced with is a test (you may want to revert to the chapter on testing you). Your wife may simply be asking you in nonverbal ways, "Do you still love me even if I am like this?" And your answer *must be* a resounding yes! in every action and every fiber of your being. But this yes is a process, not a single event. It begins by courting her, and it requires the simple discipline we previously described. What you must do is at least one thing for her each day for a year. That's all. Set up some arbitrary event a year from now—an anniversary, a birthday, or whatever; it doesn't matter. To prepare for that event you will need to begin working for it. Do not put it off until the week before or, like you do with flowers on Valentine's Day, until the drive home from work that day! Start by building a planner that has you do one thing each day in preparation for the event. It is really simple: if you are focusing on her, even for just a minute or two each day for a year, you will not only fall madly in love with your woman, the object of your focus, but you will, in the process begin seeing her in an entirely different light. Things that might have annoyed you, take on endearing qualities; she looks slimmer, and her skin seems more radiant. And guess what, you start treating her differently, and she will respond in kind.

> Take time off to be a couple together – we would take time for just us without the kids. Sometimes weekends, sometimes 4-5 days together. But don't do business in the bedroom – have a lunch date and make your financial decisions there.

Another Story from Kris: Quite some time ago, I took a series of personal empowerment programs, and one of the trainers, Jim Cook, used to tell a story from long ago in tribal Africa or India (it really doesn't matter). With thanks to Jim, I want to pass it on as I remember it. It is a story called "The Nine-Cow Woman."

The Nine-Cow Woman

A young warrior wanted to leave the tribe and build wealth and a kingdom of his own, so he approached the tribe's king to get his blessing and advice. The king liked the young man, so he gave him several pointers for his life ahead. He told him how to plan a village and that he would have to have enough farmland to support the people and animals. The king also told him that he would have to take a wife, but to do so would take a fine payment of several head of cattle.

The warrior took in all the advice from the king. "When the times comes, may I purchase one of your daughters to start a family?" he asked. The buying of women was the way of the tribes in that place long ago, and cattle were the primary means of barter.

The king had always liked the young man, and was impressed with his plans. "Absolutely," the king responded enthusiastically. "Get your village built, raise some cattle, then come back to see me. I have many daughters, and I will give you a good value for your money."

After a few years, the young warrior arrived at the king's hut with a small herd of cattle, indicating that he was ready to purchase a wife. "Take your pick; all of my daughters are over there, in that special maidens' hut."

After a short while, the warrior returned, bringing with him a young woman who stood in ragged clothes, bent over, and dirty. "This is the woman I wish to purchase, Your Highness," he said. "And I will offer you nine cows for her."

The king was taken aback. "Are you mad? Of all the daughters I have, this one is the most miserable and disagreeable. She is always frowning and moody; she does not sing nor does she dress well. She is certainly not worth nine cows! Two, three cows at best, but not nine cows."

"Sire," said the young man, "I know what I am doing. I insist on giving you nine cows for her. She will be my queen."

Reluctantly, the king accepted the offer, insisting that the younger man deliver the payment in increments of two or three cows at a time. "I do not want anyone to know that I charged you so much for such a miserable bride." The young man made his payment, and took the woman back to his village.

Several years later, the king went out traveling to see the surrounding lands, to assess how things were progressing and to gather knowledge of his people. Along his way, he happened upon the village built by the young warrior and was immediately impressed with all the prosperity and upbeat mood there. He couldn't help notice a beautiful woman walking among the townspeople, head held high, smiling broadly, kindly stopping to greet each person, especially the children. Her benevolence, warmth, and energy were clearly spreading to those around her. "I see you are doing well, son," said the king. "And that woman — she's absolutely beautiful. She must be your new queen. I am so glad you came to your senses and hid my daughter away. Who is this lovely woman?"

"Forgive me, Sire," the young Lord replied, "but that is your daughter."

"My ugly daughter — the one you paid so much for?" the king exclaimed.

"I always saw her as so much more, Sire, she was always beautiful to me" said the younger man. "And when I treated her like she had greater value, she became a queen. She's my nine-cow wife. And she was never anything less, in my eyes."

HAPPINESS AND THE FREEDOM OF CHOICE

Least you think that this is just some cutsie myth, we offer the following evidence. There is a professor at Harvard by the name of Dan Gilbert[44] who has done a huge amount of research on happiness and whose findings might shed some light on the issues of happiness in marriage. It is something that every married man should know and it goes something like this.

Gilbert reports on two studies that have direct correlation to committed marriage. In one study people were asked to rank order six Monet prints from most liked (1) to least liked (6). They then were told that, as participants, they could have one of the prints as a gift but unfortunately, the researcher only had the third- and fourth-ranked prints. Of course, the people almost invariably picked the third over the fourth. That is not the interesting part. Sometime later, those same people were asked to rank the same six prints again, and guess what? Their formerly third-ranked print came in among the top averaging a little better than second overall.

---

44 Gilbert's research is available on www.ted.com or through his blog site: http://www.randomhouse.com/kvpa/gilbert/blog/

And the formerly fourth-ranked print fell lower in the pick averaging about fifth. Being stuck with what we think is average changes our perception of our liking of that choice over time. Hmmm!

In the second study, students at Harvard were in a basic photography course where they were taught how to shoot good pictures and then, after making a contact sheet of their best efforts, were asked to pick their absolute favorite two. The students were then taught all about developing and printmaking to give their very best effort to creating two blowups of those pictures. Half were then told that they had to choose only one picture to keep and that the other was to be shipped off immediately to research headquarters in England never to be seen by them again. The other half were told to select one but that they had four days to reconsider their choice and could swap it out if they wished. The results were rather astounding. The unchangeable group when surveyed in the short term and over the long term were extremely proud and happy with their picture, while those who had a choice, when measured during the four days of consideration, shortly after their final choice point, and over the long haul, showed increasing unhappiness and displeasure with their choice!

> I never spend any energy, time or attention wondering about whether I should be here or not. I am in, I ain't going anywhere.

As an epilogue to his study, Gilbert offered students a choice in photography courses in a recent semester. In one course, they would have a reversible choice on the pictures they produced and in the other the choice would be final and irreversible. Not too surprisingly, over 66 percent of the students said that they would prefer to have a choice—or in Gilbert's words, two-thirds of us would prefer conditions in life that would make us miserable!

Translating these research studies to marriage we would contend that if and when you marry with a sense of finality and irreversibility, you actually are producing a greater possibility of happiness than if you believe that you could get divorced if it doesn't work out. Furthermore, having made that choice even in the face of the fact that there are other more attractive possibilities out there, the choosing itself increases the attractiveness of our life partner. So you see, the Nine-Cow Wife is not myth after all!

As psychologist Barry Schwartz says, "What we don't realize is that the very option of being allowed to change our minds seems to increase the chances that we *will* change our minds."[45] He goes on:

> Finding a life partner is not a matter of comparison shopping and "trading up." The only way to find happiness and stability in the presence of seemingly attractive and tempting options is to say, "I'm not going there. I've made my decision about a life partner, so this person's empathy or that person's looks have nothing to do with me. I'm not in the market—end of story." Agonizing over whether your love is "the real thing" or your sexual relationship is above or below par, and wondering if you could have done better is a prescription for misery. Knowing that you have made a choice that you will not reverse allows you to pour your energy into improving the relationship that you have rather than second-guessing it.[46]

It is a universal law—from Gandhi's single decision and the legend of The Nine-Cow Wife, to Gilbert's and Schwartz's irreversible choice—making your marriage decision a final and nonnegotiable standard of your life—one of your terms, as it were—has a profoundly positive effect on you and your marriage. That can only rub off, in a very positive way, on your spouse. Trust us, she

45 Barry Schwartz, *The Paradox of Choice, Why More is Less*, Harper Perennial, New York, NY, 2004, p. 228

46 Ibid., p. 229.

will start looking better, sounding nicer, and acting like the queen she is and has always wanted to be!

It is all up to you.

Survival Tip: No affairs, except the affair you have with your own wife. Remember how to seduce her.

SECTION 7

STAYING FIT

"There's a difference between interest and commitment. When you're interested in doing something, you do it only when it's convenient. When you're committed to something, you accept no excuses; only results."

Kenneth Blanchard

There is a sign near each of the trailheads in the Presidential Range of the White Mountains that reads: "The area ahead has the worst weather in North America. Do not go further unless you have extra food and clothing and are in top physical condition." Venturing into marriage, like hiking in the wilderness, requires that you stay fit and conditioned.

(Dave and Kris)

YOUR MARRIAGE FITNESS ROUTINE

Do you have a physical fitness routine? You know: three days a week in the gym; running a couple of miles each day; sit-ups and push-ups daily. Do you belong to a club or take Tae Kwon Do or something like that? You do it and follow it religiously so that you will live longer and feel better for the rest of your life and so that you can be there for your family for a long time to come.

Your marriage skills need a fitness routine as well. Throughout this guide, we have outlined elements of that fitness routine. Those disciplines need to be practiced with the same rigor as your fitness routine. If you don't have a fitness routine, you get fat, short of breath, and die young. If you don't have a marriage fitness routine, your marriage, falls into disrepair, gets sloppy, and dies an untimely and unhappy death. As a review, here are some of the exercise stations already outlined in this guide:

- Listening—spend at least half of the time you are with your wife just listening to her. Listen to what she says and listen to what she does not say—especially listen to the "why" of what she says. Get good at listening.

- Fifteen minutes of focused uninterrupted time with her each day. If you find yourself surfing the net, stop, turn off the computer and go focus on her (same for porn, vegging out, or any other distraction that isn't your personal time). Make unproductive time productive by focusing on her.

- Personal time—you need some personal reflection time for yourself as well. (This is not surfing for porn.) You give her fifteen minutes of focused time, don't skimp on your fifteen minutes either. If you can't meditate, go for a walk or just sit and think, but this is just time for you. Go to the well and refresh yourself.

- Meet with your men regularly and open yourself to being regularly "inspected" by them. Being on a men's team is a fitness routine. You cannot see the back of your head so get some help.

- Find a marriage mentor—an elder with many years of successful, happy marriage under his belt—then shut up and listen to what he has to say. Remember, even Michael Phelps has a coach.

- Know your terms and regularly check to see that you are living up to your established standard of who you say you are.

Get in shape and stay in shape. It is a matter of discipline and regularity.

SUN TZU AND *THE ART OF WAR*[47]

Y ou may wonder why we chose to write about the "art of war" in this guide on relationship success. The simple truth is that men can relate to warring and battles. In addition, we need to recognize that for over 2,500 years *The Art of War* has stood as one of the most circulated and universally used pieces of "relationship" wisdom on the planet. We would wager that you could go into the sales office of any major corporation in the country and find at least one copy of Master Sun's wisdom on the shelf there. Sun Tzu was a master of the craft of engaging with others for the successful resolution of conflicts that arise between two people, two factions, or two nations.

Master Sun laid out five principles in mastering these conflicts. They were: 1) Tao (righteousness or ethics); 2) Tien (timing); 3) Di (resources, including location); 4) Jiang (leadership); and 5) Fa (execution and follow-through). As a man in relationship, you would be

---

47 There are numerous translations and commentaries on The *Art of War*, one of the most widely read books in history, but the best translation we've found actually comes from Chin-Ning Chu, *The Art of War for Women*, Random House/Currency Books, New York, NY, 2007.

well advised to listen to the wisdom of this ancient master. Applied to the art of relating to your wife and winning in the long-term engagement of marriage, there is much from which you could benefit.

Tao. The word Tao roughly translates in English as "the way." It is used to refer to the way of heaven, the way of the universe, and the nature of all things. The first and foremost principle of winning concerns righteousness, morals, and ethics. You must always—in all aspects of your relationship with your wife—operate from a well-founded code of ethics. Ask yourself if you have a Code of Honor or a clearly defined set of moral principles at your foundation. If you cannot recite them, it is likely that you do not. It is not sufficient to "think" that you have a moral underpinning. You need to know them, memorize them, and act only from that base.

Embedded within this concept is a sense of the ultimate wholeness or oneness of all things. In Tao are both male and female, right and wrong, good and bad, real and imaginary. These things are inextricable from each other. There cannot be masculinity without femininity, right without wrong. A good choice on one day may be bad on another—both are contained in each other. It is for that reason that Sun Tzu built his leadership principles on the requirement of a strong moral ethic. He understood that this principle demanded that the leader inspect the current action in the context of the ultimate outcome. In your marriage, and in each encounter with your woman, you are challenged to ask yourself, "How righteous is my objective?" Is your action being driven by your ego or by your neediness? If so, just check it at the door when you come home—it has no place in your relationship.

Tien. Timing, they say, is everything. Or to quote Ecclesiastes, "To everything there is a season and a time for every purpose under heaven." In relationship, as in battle, timing makes all the difference between success and failure, between winning and losing. Master Sun taught that there are two kinds of tien, personal timing and universal timing. Personal timing is your agenda—the idea that certain things should happen in a certain order or by a certain time in your life, or they are unacceptable. Universal timing is the natural rhythm and flow of all things. Sun Tzu says the goal is always to align your time with universal time and to be in harmony with the flow. If you are exerting effort in making your case or in pushing a cause, most likely you are out of sync with universal time.

In relationship, this means that you need to exercise judgment when engaging with your spouse. There may be a particular issue you do need to bring up but knowing when to "pop the question" is critical. Your ego can suck you into something that is best left to another time. You may have to ripen your thoughts before they are ready to harvest, and other times you may want to just plant the seed for something to grow that may not even be ready for months. Sometimes it may be best in a heated discussion to lay out an idea and allow it time to percolate, but not drive for the "close" at that time.

Timing in the positive arena must be exercised equally as prudently. If she rejects some gift or request for sexual intimacy, it might not be you she is rejecting, but rather your timing. Always ask yourself if you are practicing Tien—universal timing or personal timing. Timing is everything.

Di. The concept of Di has to do with your resources. What personal and physical resources do you have at your disposal? Think of these as the tools in your toolbox. Some of you may be supremely articulate and capable of running circles around your wife in any battle of wits. Some of you are skilled with your hands or in physicality. Remember that a given resource can be at different times either an asset or a liability. Sun Tzu always pointed out that our goal is to be aware of that and turn our liabilities into assets.

But by resources, Sun also was referring to location and the lay of the land—prime considerations in planning battles. Do you have arguments in your bedroom or bathroom? Where is the neutral location in your home so that your wife does not feel trapped when "attacked" by you? It is as important to consider her sense of the location as well. If your objective is to subdue the enemy, that is one thing but if your righteous objective is sustaining the relationship, then be aware of the "lay of the land" when you choose to engage with her. Sometimes a surprise amorous attack in the kitchen produces a surprising result, and sometimes suggesting the use of some "toy," hours into a passionate lovemaking session can instantly deflate her desire. Like Tien (timing), your resources are essential tools for success when used judiciously and in the proper fashion.

Jing. One of the most referred-to and yet misunderstood of Master Sun's principles is Jing or *Leadership*. How well are you leading in this relationship? Believe it or not, your wife wants your leadership—she really wants to know where you want to take the marriage so that she will be able to work her relationship magic in making it happen. However, this is not an invitation to have it your way. In Sun Tzu's world, a leader was the one who led through the will of the people. As his contemporary, Lao Tzu (translated simply as "Old Man"), the author of the Tao de Ching, said, "The greatest leader is the one of whom the people said, 'we did it ourselves.'"

Sun Tzu said that a leader must be wise, trustful, benevolent, courageous, and disciplined. That's a tall order. You need to step up to the plate in leading this family, but it is not a matter of authoritative leadership, nor is it a suggestion to lead by example. It is the wise *way* that you decide, which shows that you are always moving from and for the common good of the family, that will give her a sense of your good leadership. Take the lead, and take it clearly and powerfully, but take it with all the humility and generosity you can muster. It may be better to not take the lead than to barge ahead without thinking, or to make a waffling decision. And in all of your leadership, you must be disciplined; a state that requires your constant training and shaping of your will and your being.

Fa (managing execution). Managing the execution is essential in managing her understanding of who you really are. Even if you say something as trivial as, "Sure, I'll take out the trash," then do it—now—not later. Be your words! She will know what you really are by what you do and not by what you say. We always tell our men, if you want to know what a man really believes, look at where he is standing! Don't tell us that your family is important if you are continually at the office at eight o'clock every night!

This means knowing what your priorities are and acting accordingly. Fa is all about taking the right action. An old Chinese proverb says, "Many a man's house has burned to the ground while the owner chased after the arsonist!" Who cares who is to blame? Act and follow through on your actions and commitments. Do everything you do all the way to the end, completing the task. How many half-finished projects are cluttering up your house and your relationship? How many promises have you not fulfilled? It may be time to sit down and make a list, committing to knock off one thing each week.

Survival Tip: Practice the five elements: be righteous, on universal time, know where and what you have, lead in the relationship and follow through to completion. It's a tall order but the best instruction you can get.

THE PERFECT MARRIAGE

There seems to be some myth in our society—long perpetuated by Disney or some TV channel—that the perfect marriage would be one of bliss and pure harmony. This myth would have us believe that two opposites perfectly complement each other and that the dynamic tension of yin and yang results in a complete whole that is perfect, stable, and wondrous.

Poppycock!

As far as we can tell, there are two flaws with this myth:

1. That when a man and a woman come together in an effort to find their "completion" in the other, it is flawed to begin with. The only chance you have at having a healthy marriage is first to be complete and wholly self-sufficient from the start. Trying to build a marriage on the hopes that your other half will be all that you should be in the first place will place an unrealistic and impossible demand on your partner. If you *did* get married with gaps and missing elements in your development (which was a serious mistake), you need to work on those with your men, with your therapist or on your own—but NOT with your wife. It is unfair and a surefire formula for disaster!

2. That any two people—even if they were identical twins with the same history and experiential upbringing—would see everything the same way and have no blips, bumps, and upsets, is not only illogical but purely ludicrous. Hey, most people marry their opposites—that's what we like about them—they are not only the opposite gender, they are often opposite on many dimensions of experience, thought, and beliefs. That is what makes this adventure exciting and adventurous.

So, we actually have to start with that assumption. The perfect marriage will always be a joining of opposites—man and woman[48*]—and therefore is one fraught with differences: differences in opinion, decision-making styles, emotions, processes, biology, brain chemistry—you name it. That is the spice—that is what makes it juicy and challenging and absolutely, positively wonderful. As men we delight in challenges—we even challenge ourselves, tossing a wad of paper into the wastebasket. Were our wives not a challenge, we are certain that men would all eventually get bored and seek the challenge—or the chase—somewhere else (have you ever seen that happen?—only a thousand times or more!). We thrive under these conditions and we wither up and become impotent without them. So stop complaining and start embracing the differences. But that is just the starting point.

> I am not so committed to being in love with the woman that I married but I am totally committed to being in love with my marriage.

The perfect marriage is one that develops a methodology of resolving and dealing with these differences. We call it "workability." The perfect marriage is more committed to working things out

---

48* We both celebrate the states that have finally recognized the naturalness of same-sex marriages, but since neither of us knows what it is like to be married to our own gender and since our mentors have also been heterosexual, we must limit our discussion to what we know. Someone else will have to write that book.

than to being right. Fall in love with the differences your woman presents you with. You may actually be nearly dead opposites on any given personality test. Who knows and who cares? But when it works, it is spectacular. For example, let's say your wife is a details person and you are a big picture person. When traveling, she gets the new city's subway transit flat in a matter of seconds, while you may emerge from the underground, look for the sun and key land-marks and know where you are instantly. It is a great combination. However those same differences can often become the source of great disagreements when she has noticed some small (almost un-noticeable) fact or speck of minutia and you pick up on a theme of which she has no awareness.

People can approach logic in two fundamentally opposite di-rections—either from how things differ from each other, or from how things are similar. These differences are not the only problems we encounter. But working out these differences and disagreements can become the success formula for your marriage. Remember, your wife is a woman. She thinks like one, has abandonment issues like other women, has body-image concerns that invariably affect your relationship and intimacy potential—all of that. It is not a prob-lem, but rather the source of your differences. You need to find a way to live with each other's differences, support those differences, and allow each other to grow and develop in different ways and even in different directions, if necessary.

You must work out all of those differing needs and directions. To have a successful and vibrant marriage, work on them; do not ignore or dismiss them. Beyond that, however, you will also need to find a productive way to call arguments into being when needed— to start the arguments. That being so, you will also need to find a way to intervene within arguments in ways that either grant a time-out or that call attention to when one or the other of you is getting overly ego-positioned. With these two additional tools, you will be able to disagree more productively.

In the beginning of his current marriage, Kris was afraid that getting into an argument would lead to certain disaster, having painfully failed at arguments and two marriages before. But when he approached disagreements from his commitments to his wife, the marriage, and "workability," he discovered that just the opposite happened—they dealt with their differences in ways that enhanced the relationship, and have now built a long legacy of problems that they have overcome, solved, or worked through.

The lesson is that when couples can enter into heated, positioned arguments and successfully resolve those problems and differences, they begin to build up a pile of evidence that the relationship can survive such threats and assaults. Kris and his wife have now over nineteen years of evidence that their loving and relationship are bigger than any disagreement they can have and that they can work through any problem they encounter. And with that, Kris no longer cringes when she says, "We've gotta talk!"

THAT is the perfect marriage!

GROWING OLD TOGETHER

You are getting older—it is something we humans do! And, by the way, the alternatives—either plastic surgery or death—both suck! But we could probably predict that you and your wife have not taken time to talk about your vision of growing old together. As a result, all you have for a reference point is either your memories of "the way we were" or the growing body of glam shots (from the Internet) of others who are younger, wealthier, or more popular than you. As we have said, those comparisons make anything "less than" appear "worse than."

This is uncharted territory for most of us. Other than creating either death wills or living wills, most couples don't take the time to create their vision of aging. Of course, there are the obvious physical aspects of growing old: you will have less strength and versatility; you will add a few minutes to your personal best running time (if you continue running at all); you both will gain weight in places you don't want it and lose mass in places you do; she will get droopy boobs; her ass will widen; through menopause she will probably be dryer in those vital juicy parts; her voice will lower; her desire for sex will perhaps slacken a bit. Look—when you were

> One of our men, who is married 43 years to a woman whose health is now failing, had this advice: "The other night just as I was falling asleep, my wife asked, 'Would you get me a drink of water?' It took everything I could muster to pull myself back from almost asleep, but I got up and got her a glass. It may not be advice – but it's what works."

younger, you believed you were immortal, you thought that if you paid your dues and worked hard, you would be somehow honored and rewarded with vigorous old age or immortality. If you are focusing on the physiology of aging and comparing it to your youthful memories of all-nighter sex marathons, you are in for a saddening downturn. But the lessons of aging and the values of the wisdom journey both men and women go through are far more wonderful.

Maybe you were lucky and had a model of aging relationships that you admired—grandparents or neighbors—but we can almost bet that you didn't talk it over when you two were courting and that you haven't done a thing about it since. Faced with less than half of your living years left to go (and each day shrinks that reserve further), you must decide how you are going to value your time together. You don't need any more reasons why this is important—this is your partner, your woman, your choice—the choice that never has to be reconsidered. So let's get to the business of creating a vision.

What can you two anticipate? What do you want to do about those things? The only things you will find on the Web or in bookstores are either poems or financial planning texts. So you really have to trust each other and make this one up.

1. Both of you will change your interests over time, so how will you allow for those changes and differences in direction? What keeps you active and alive may be something other than what keeps her engaged and excited. Don't try to anticipate *what* those things are, but *how* you will allow and encourage each other to pursue them—to venture fur-

ther and further from home and still want and be able to return to that home port of call.

2. Do a visioning exercise—together! Despite your differing growth areas, you need some things that draw you together. Sit down and start talking about creating some future vision of what you want to do together as elders. This might be to become Peace Corps volunteers in Malawi or to travel the world and see all the sights you wanted to see. Dream big or dream little (a garden out back where you both can work)—it really doesn't matter.

3. Take care of each other physically. Start looking at your diet and invest in your future by eating well. Start taking brisk morning walks together or jogging together (remember this is not a competition so stay with her). Or get into yoga; it is a routine that can age with you.

4. As injuries and age take their tolls on your bodies and limit your ranges of motion or capacities, adapt your living space accordingly. The key is to walk the line between aggressive recovery through physical therapy and scaling back to accommodate the loss that may never be regained.

5. Above all, don't wait until you're both too old either to start these or to begin enjoying some of them. How many stories do you know of where the guy retired and then died within six months, having only stepped into that Florida condo the one time when he bought it?

STUDY YOUR WOMAN

Patton studied Rommel. Fischer studied Spasky. You study Tae Kwon Do, or fantasy football league stats, or whatever. Anyone who ever wanted to be great in his craft studied it as a practice. And you must study your wife. It is the only way to be powerful in your relationship and to have even half a chance at moving from surviving to thriving in marriage. But how?

You live with her, right? So wake up and pay attention. Notice her habits, how she goes about her day, what she chooses when nobody is watching. You need to become a student of this woman. Here is a short list of what you might consider as the required study areas for this new expertise you are going to build:

- First and foremost, ask her what her favorite things are. And another ask her what is really important to her. Keep interviewing her like you did on initial approach.
- Ask her woman friends what she likes and dislikes. They know a part of her that you may never see, or that she may be too nice to discuss with you.
- Look through her memorabilia—you know, photo albums,

scrapbooks, and the like. Does she have a drawer with keepsakes in it? If you don't feel like it is a violation of "off-limits" territory, look through it and get a new look at your woman. Or better yet, look through it together with her.

- Take notice of what she wears both when she dresses up for an occasion and when she dresses down to relax.
- What does she do to unwind? Where is her favorite place to go?
- We realize we repeat this *ad nauseam*, but listen to what she talks about. And here is what you should do with it—look for the pattern. What do all these themes suggest when taken as a group?
- What else could you study?

WHAT WOMEN WANT FROM US MEN (WITH A LITTLE HELP FROM OUR WIVES)

While we are at it, let's pass on a few pointers about what you might find out when you take the time to study your woman. Women actually would like to see more of (or at least some of) certain things in their men. By no means is this an exhaustive list, but think of it as a starter kit:

- Ask her opinion. Throughout this guide, we have repeatedly said that you need to listen. But you need to ask her what she wants and needs. It not only starts the conversation going, it actually validates her in the process.

- Own your territory and expand it (responsibly). You need to keep your stuff in order and do your tasks around the house. But beyond that, take on new elements of house maintenance (cleaning, fixing, and streamlining). Help her out with the stupid and mundane tasks—dishes, laundry, or anything like it will do just fine. Bottom line: she doesn't need another kid to take care of—ask, "How can I help you?" with regularity.

- Learn about what works in relationships. We strongly recommend that you read Chapman's *The Five Love Languages (Men's Edition)*,[49] then talk about it with her. You don't have to be a scholar or get into psychology, just ask her what she thinks might be her love language or what she thinks yours might be. Then, having recognized that about her, ask what a good thing might be for you to do. This is not rocket science, brothers!

- Make mistakes and admit them. Hey we don't even care if you make mistakes on purpose; it's the admitting ("Gee, honey, I really made a mistake there!") that counts. Understand that your woman wants to see you being aware and responsible for your screwups as well as your successes.

- Get active in a charity. Sponsor an animal at the Heifer Project, volunteer at the senior center, or read books to kids at the library—whatever! Just get off your duff and give up an hour of football to do good for others. (Women really dig that.)

- Stay active with a men's team. Actually, our women want us to go to the men. We get things there that they cannot give us. And it hopefully prevents us from thinking we can treat her like a man.

- They're your offspring too. Is your wife doing all the childrearing (caring for the baby all day and, when you come home all tired from work, still having to keep the little tyke out of your hair; being the one to make lunches and pack them off on the bus only to have to leave her job early to get them from school to the dentist or home from soccer practice)? Make sure you give her a night or two off.

---

49 Gary Chapman, *The Five Love Languages, Men's Edition*, Northfield Publishing, Chicago, IL, 2004.

Raising children is a lot of work, and just as hard as the job you do—but with kids you have to be "on" all the time.

- Care about what she cares about. (Ask her again.) This applies to daily living as well as vacation time. Make sure you split up the vacation to have some stuff for her or do alternate vacations (one for her and one for you).

We began this guide saying that we really don't know much about women—and we know even less about your woman. Individuals never fit general patterns, so you need to become the expert on her.

This is where we will have to depart and turn it over to you. We can't be with you at the next turn in the road, and we can only write so much before we get tired of hearing our own voices. The rest will have to be up to you. You have the tools; you know what you need to do. Our fervent hope is that you do it all and more, and that the next chapter will be written by you.

Good luck
Kris and Dave

SECTION 8

250 GREAT THINGS TO DO
(TO KEEP HER SMILING)

*"A successful marriage requires falling in love many times,
always with the same person."*

Mignon McLaughlin

A List of 250 Things That Could Make Her Happy and Keep Her Smiling

(Thanks to our men's teams)

You have a new job: you need to focus on your courtship skills and how they can delight your wife. You must do all you can (despite what you think and feel and despite her current state) to make her happy. It is how you got here. It is your duty, your job, your requirement. This is not an option that you can do when you remember it or when YOU feel like it. It is a must, and what it *must* become is a habit. Develop the habit of courting your wife and bringing a smile to her face and you will have mastered one of the great challenges in married life. Just do it.

What follows here is a list we hope you will find interesting. But there are a couple of rules you need to be aware of before beginning. First, not all of these will work for every woman. Women are unique and different, so some like one type of courtship while others are wooed quite differently.

Second, WOMEN did not develop this list. It was developed by men for men. As such, it does not reflect women's attitudes and may not necessarily be what they want and like. This list reflects what has worked for a whole bunch of men across a whole hell of a lot of time and women—in long-term, committed, monogamous, heterosexual relationships.

Third, you must do these things clandestinely. If it is seen that you are in any way engaging in these actions from any position of self-seeking, you are serving yourself, not your wife, and that little issue will bleed all over your good intentions. But most importantly, you have to do these things because you want to and because you love and adore your woman. Your goal is to make her smile, to bring her happiness, and joy. The goal of this practice is NOT to get you laid! If that happens because she is happier, well good for you; you got lucky! The goal is to keep her happy, cuz, as they say, "When Momma ain't happy, ain't nobody happy!"

So have fun with the list and get in the habit of doing something every day or three times a week, and then start adding your own.

Remember from the Relationship Equity Account section that everything you do is worth 1 point. The discipline is to deposit regularly and often. Most importantly, HAVE FUN! Make it up. Try and fail and then try again!

WARNING: the following ideas are provided for you to be able to build a discipline of courting your woman and are not intended to be used as "fix-it" tools should she be in a bad mood. In fact, if you try to assuage her anger by whipping up one of these, you have missed the whole point of this guide. Go back and read and practice more.

So how do you make her feel special? Let's go!

1.   Clean/wash/wax her car—detail it better than yours!

2.   Hang an "I Love You" note in the refrigerator.

3.   Write "I Love You" backward in soap on the rear window of her car so she reads it in the mirror.

4.   Buy her flowers for no reason at all.

5.   Give her a massage with self-warming oil by candlelight.

6.   Hide love notes around the house (her underwear drawer works well).

7.   Write her a poem (corny is OK).

8.   Each month for the next twelve months focus on paying attention to a different part of her body. Give little massages there, stroke that part, buy gifts for that part, etc. (NOTE: Do not start with her breasts—show some class and save

that for one of the last. Start with her feet or hands or arms, and see how long it takes for her to figure out what you are doing!)

9. Make her cell phone's ring tone her favorite song or "your song."

10. Scan in a wedding picture and make it her screen saver.

11. Have your men's team cater a surprise dinner at your house (for no reason at all).

12. Put the flowers in a vase.

13. Watch 9½ *Weeks* together. We have it on good authority that this is the most breathtaking passion-arousing movie for women to watch—and better than any pornography.

14. Sometime later, you might want to get a copy of *Joe Cocker's Greatest Hits* CD and set up and reenact the *Leave Your Hat On* scene!

15. Watch any romance classic (chick flick) together (*Casablanca* with Bogart and Bacall, *From Here to Eternity*, or *Swept Away* work nicely, but you choose).

16. Send a card, for no particular occasion.

17. Remind her of special days before she reminds you.

18. One rose is more romantic than a dozen.

19. Write a new verse to "your song." If you don't have a "your song," pick a sappy love song out and tell her why it reminds you of the two of you.

20. Surprise her with a treasure hunt with your kids on Mother's Day. Have the kids make little presents—drawings or origami, etc.—and hide them around the house with clues to the location of the next present.

21. Notice a little thing she did for one of the kids, and thank her for it in bed that night.

22. Sneak into the shower with her.

23. Put stick-on tattoos on each other.

24. Rent a limousine and take her out in style some night. Have her picked up first.

25. Body-paint each other—make henna tattoos with her.

26. Make love and agree to talk dirty to each other (like in the porn flicks).

27. Specifically Praise and Compliment.

28. Read her a poem—reciting one is even better—saying it reminds you of her.

29. Ask her questions about what she's interested in.

30. Be in touch with one of her old friends; arrange a surprise call or get-together.

31. Bring in surprise takeout for dinner.

32. Go away for a night together.

33. Arrange a surprise date (day or night).

34. Pretend you both speak a different language and are from different planets.

35. Make love without using real words.

36. Buy some sidewalk chalk and write a love note in her parking space.

37. With the same chalk write "WELCOME TO THE HOME OF THE MOST LOVED AND ADORED WOMAN IN TOWN" on the sidewalk or driveway when you have a

bunch of people coming over to the house (watch her face when people keep mentioning how nice it must be—and she hasn't a clue why).

38.   Ogle her while she gets dressed in the morning.

39.   Show up at her work with flowers (hand-deliver them).

40.   When she reads a magazine and sniffs the perfume, ask for the name of it and buy it.

41.   Every time she says she doesn't feel like cooking, offer to get takeout—or cook if you can.

42.   Take a cooking class on the sly and prepare the best thing that you learned from the class—just for her.

43.   Call her in the middle of the day and say, "Remember that time we were…It reminded me of how much I love you, and I had to call you."

44. Thank her for something (anything, actually!).

45. Tell her you appreciate her for...(make sure it was not for something she just did).

46. Send her a sappy text message on her cell phone or e-mail her at work.

47. When she says, "That sounds really good," immediately do it.

48. Offer to brush her hair.

49. Take something heavy out of her hands and bring it to its destination.

50. Carry in the groceries. (Always)

51. Do the laundry, especially your ripe sweats and grubbies (careful with doing hers, dude; wool shrinks in hot water, colors fade, and fine things like stockings have to be washed by hand

or in the little mesh bag you might find somewhere around her stocking or bra drawer).

52. Open the car door for her in public.

53. Compliment her in front of her friends.

54. Do something for her parents.

55. Change the desktop of her computer to something pretty.

56. Buy her a gift certificate for the salon.

57. Lock the kids out of the house for an hour or if they are younger have them go play at the neighbor's house for an hour.

58. Leave her a love note on the table before she gets up.

59. Show up with a coffee from her favorite coffee shop.

60. Leave her a brochure from a faraway land.

61. Drop her off in front of your destination when it is raining, and then park the car.

62. Come home early and make dinner.

63. Talk about her to your men, in front of her.

64. Tell her how beautiful she is.

65. Tell her how lucky you are.

66. Bring home chocolates.

67. Hold her hand in public.

68. When prompted, let her know why she is better than the beautiful woman you were caught looking at.

69. Make her an herbal tea.

70. Give her a footbath.

71. Ask her a question that you know she is good at answering. ("What color curtains look better in here?").

72. Praise HER children.

73. Compliment her in front of her children.

74. Offer to drop her off at Barnes & Noble for an hour.

75. Ask her to pick out the clothes you should wear to work.

76. Kiss her on the nape of her neck when she least expects it.

77. Whistle at her.

78.   Grab yourself and ask her to step away so you can calm that thing down.

79.   Turn the clock back an hour and ask to spend more time with her.

80.   Put a dish of rose petals by her bedside.

81.   Pick up a *Cosmopolitan* and bring it home.

82.   Buy some crazy tropical fruit and share it with her.

83.   Put the seat down on the toilet and joke about it.

84.   Loudly tell her you love her when she is talking on the phone to someone else.

85.   Balance her checkbook.

86. Buy a rubber ink stamp and give each other matching tattoos.

87. Draw a picture of the both of you in a special place and frame it.

88. Tell her you don't deserve her.

89. Write her a list of reasons why you are grateful to have her.

90. Talk to her about faraway places SHE wants to see.

91. Ask her about what a ceremony to renew your vows would look like.

92. Get her name engraved on something.

93. Request your wedding song from the DJ when you go out (make sure he mentions her name).

94. Ask her to dance whenever you hear music.

95. Try to sing her a song.

96. Make your own card and give it to her.

97. Win her a prize at the park.

98. Send her flowers or chocolates with a card from "A Secret Admirer," and deny it if she asks.

99. Have your men call and, if she answers, compliment her before asking for you.

100. Pay her Victoria's Secret charge card bill for a month.

101. Draw a heart on her paper plate before she puts food in it.

102. Read her fortune cookie, but make up something great.

103. Read your fortune cookie, and compliment her through it.

104. Have Mall Services page her, and be waiting with a gift.

105. Make a scene in a restaurant screaming, "I LOVE MY WIFE!"

106. Find out where she is going for an errand, beat her there, purchase the item, and have the clerk give it to her.

107. Fill her gas tank.

108. Pick flowers from the side of the road and bring them home.

109. Rent a Town Car and have a buddy show up as your chauffeur to drive you wherever you want all night long: a bar, then a stroll in the park, then ice cream near the beach—just have fun with it.

110. Offer to go for a walk with her. LISTEN, no talking.

111. Explain why your marriage is better than the TV show marriage you're watching.

112.   Get a caricature done of the both of you.

113.   Frame, display, and preserve anything she gives you.

114.   Pay for a manicure, pedicure, nails, etc.

115.   Change your cell phone voice mail message to say something sweet, and then have your wife call you.

116.   When she calls you on the phone, say something like, "Be still my beating heart."

117.   Ask her often, "How is the most beautiful woman in the world doing?"

118.   If she offers sex, tell you are not worthy enough to be with such a woman.

119.   Get His/Hers whatever.

120. Call her on the phone and tell her that you have the wrong number, that you were calling someone old, fat, and ugly.

121. This one is expensive but works great. Deliver her flowers on the hour every hour for five hours—it really works

122. Offer to wash her back in the tub.

123. Buy tub salts/bubbles, etc.

124. Light a candle.

125. Hell, buy her one of every sample at the candle shop.

126. Listen for her favorite choice, and then buy her a big one.

127. Write I love...on cardboard, and put it on her door (car, work, and bedroom).

128. Call her best friend and tell her it is going great between you and your woman.

129. When you come back from a team meeting, tell her that you learned how much you appreciate her, etc.

130. Buy her a queen's crown at the party store. Make up some great stuff here (she is the Queen of the Nile; she is the Queen of your world; she is your Queen and you are her man-servant/page/whatever). Make her wear it.

131. Interrupt someone you don't know (in the park, supermarket, etc.) and introduce him or her to your beautiful wife.

132. Kiss her good-bye when she is going out, then run out to the car and kiss her again. Run down the street after her and try to get a third one.

133. Have her favorite music playing on the stereo when she gets home.

134. Call her favorite radio station and request a song while she is driving to work.

135. Buy some stupid gadget, and put it in her car. Let her know that if she needs love, it will send a transmission to your cell phone, and you will call her right away. Call her every ten minutes, and tell her the transmitter keeps going off.

136. Put her wedding ring inside of yours at night. Let her know why.

137. Ask her to wear something because it pleases you.

138. Tell her she smells very nice. (Please insert many adjectives). For extra bonus points, tell her she smells nice when she isn't wearing perfume.

139. Offer to put her socks on her.

140. Tuck her in bed at night.

141. Reminisce about your wedding day/honeymoon/special occasion.

142. Dig out the wedding album and keep telling her how fantastically stupendously wonderful that day was—but that you had no idea it would turn out that well.

143. Call her mom and compliment your wife.

144. Call her mom and thank her for raising such a magnificent daughter. Tell her that it reflects on her—what a wonderful woman she is as well.

145. Compliment the people around your wife. They WILL tell her and it WILL make her feel good.

146. Be a goofball, especially with her children.

147. Let her know that her children have her eyes, smile, beautiful hair, etc.

148. Write her a check for a million dollars, and have fun talking about how you would spend it.

149. Here is a great one. Take a piece of construction paper and roll it into a cone. Put some bath beads, soap, etc. in the cone, wrap it in aluminum foil, and write a love note coming out of the tip of the cone. When you are done, it should look like a Hershey's Kiss (instant gratitude generator).

150. Make a set of rings out of pipe cleaners and ask her to marry you again for the day. Wear them all day long and show them off whenever possible.

151. Search the Internet for a recipe for a drink, bread, dessert, etc., and make it for her.

152. Learn how to make a balloon animal (it is really simple; practice with your men's team), and then make her one in front of her, or make one for her at the next party the two of you attend.

153. Make a motion as if you are going to faint the next time you hug her.

154. Moaning works too.

155. Get caught staring at her breasts (deny it), then do it again.

156. Take a picture of her and hang it where she can see it (your office desk, bedroom table, etc)—have her see you looking at it.

157. Research something romantic (constellations, Roman gods, etc.) and share it with her.

158. Learn her astrological sign, read your horoscope and hers, then tell her why she is so compatible with you.

159. Read *The Five Love Languages* by Greg Chapman—use it.

160. Find out (through experimentation) which of her five senses are most sensitive and arousing.

161. Remember, a woman's biggest and most sensitive organ is her brain; this list will enhance your luck with the rest of her body!

162. Praise her and do nice things for her in front of her friends, colleagues at work, and in other public places where others will notice her getting praise.

163. Call her boss (if she works) and arrange a personal day for her, then buy an all-expense-paid visit to the day spa she's always talked about.

164. Meet her after work for a drink or cappuccino before going home.

165. Give her a copy of David Whyte's poem *The True Love* printed on a plaque.

166. Engrave her name on a plaque and hang it in your office—make sure she knows about it.

167. Brag about her—brag about her again.

168. Keep a section of your BlackBerry/iPhone reserved for notes on anything she mentions that she likes (so you can remember when you get a chance).

169. Make a trail of sticky-notes through the house telling her how wonderful she is.

170. Create a scavenger hunt for her with a great present at the end.

171. Memorize several of Pablo Neruda's love sonnets—just plain gooood bullshit—and spontaneously recite one occasionally.

172. Offer to give her a pedicure; use soaps, scents, oils, then trim and paint her toenails.

173. Give her the greatest massage of her life and don't have it lead to anything else!

174. Build a small campfire in the backyard some night and make S'mores.

175. Ask her to reminisce with you about your first date—get the details (date, what she was wearing, you were wearing, etc.), make note of it and, at some future time, on a night out, say how you were just thinking of your first date.

176. Here's one that's a little more expensive! Schedule an impromptu weekend trip to some place special.

177. Or short of that take a weekender in NYC and do the MOMA or an off-Broadway play and dinner.

178. Easier still, sit down with her and plan a fantasy trip to somewhere exotic she would like to visit—go on Google Earth and talk about what you would do at each of the highlighted spots.

179. Play hooky and go to the beach (summer) or skiing (winter).

180. Buy some art and hang it about the house—of particular value would be Gustav Klimt's "The Kiss," or other pictures of lovers embracing or walking hand-in-hand or photos and paintings of her favorite places.

181. Name a star after her (StarRegistry.com).

182. Hire someone to come in and cook a meal for her (or the whole family).

183. Hire someone to come and clean the place—a maid, a really ugly but fastidious maid.

184. Kidnap her from work or home and take her out for an afternoon and night on the town.

185. Cancel your plans and plan to be with your wife instead.

186. Put the toilet seat down.

187. Run errands for her.

188. Go shopping with her and—patiently—sit in the "husband chair" and watch as she plays dress-up.

189. Encourage her to buy something whimsical or not needed on a shopping excursion.

190. Oooh and aaah over her purchase of the fourteenth pair of (yet once again) black shoes.

191. Agree with her (just once in a while) when she claims to have saved money by buying something because it was on sale.

192. Program your computer to e-mail her love notes at various times during the day when you are not even near the computer (under options/ check the box "do not deliver before" and set the time). I once arranged for a different romantic picture to arrive in my wife's in-box each hour on Valentine's Day when I was away conducting a seminar all day.

193. Call her at lunch to play hooky for a two-hour lunchtime rendezvous.

194. Cover the windows at night and make the room pitch black and find your way around each other's bodies.

195. Stroke her skin (especially her neck, behind the knees, or inner thighs) with silk (very lightly) or feathers.

196. Read David Deida's *Way of the Superior Man* or Wayne Levine's *Hold On To Your N.U.T.S.* They are the closest things to doing a Men's Weekend in writing that you will find, with some really great tips on this part of your relationship.

197. Immediately download or develop the pictures (at a one-hour photo shop) from your vacation so she can take them to work the next day and show off her good time.

198. Hang a sign from the bridge over the interstate where she drives proclaiming your undying commitment and love for her.

199. On your vacation at the beach, hire a skywriter to spell out some intimate, loving message to her from you or have someone deliver a love note to her.

200. Daydream with her about "someday."

201. Paint the room whatever color she wants (what the hell do you care!).

202. Bring her breakfast in bed some weekday when you have to leave early.

203. Run into the house all excited-like and drag her outside to lie in the grass and look at cloud shapes—say, "You should have

seen it—there was one just like you—it was beautiful!" Stay out there for an hour identifying more shapes and things.

204. Nominate her for "Citizen of the Week" or "Parent of the Month" or anything; just nominate her for it and make up a bunch of reasons why she should be selected.

205. Donate to her favorite cause in her name.

206. Take her to karaoke night and sing "your song" out loud to her—on one knee!

207. Take ballroom dance lessons.

208. Plant a flower or tree in her honor in your yard.

209. Ask her to snuggle on the couch.

210. Ask her to watch a sunrise or sunset together.

211. Take her for a hayride or a sleigh ride.

212. Always answer the phone if she calls, even if you are already talking on the phone.

213. Ask her to clothes shop for you.

214. Go shopping with her and enjoy it.

215. Buy her mother a present for no reason at all.

216. Build her a swinging chair in the backyard.

217. Pick up some cheap paints and paint a picture and give it to her.

218. Landscape the front or back yard.

219. Take up a sport you both can play together.

220. Learn to play bridge, spades, or her favorite game.

221. Hang out on a bridge and play "Pooh sticks" (see A.A. Milne for instructions). Each of you drops a stick over the upstream side of the bridge and then runs to the other side to see whose comes through first.

222. Buy her a kitten/puppy/etc.

223. Always shower and shave before going out to dinner with her.

224. First time you see her in the morning, tell her she looks great.

225. Don't smoke in the house or the car (especially cigars).

226. Go to bed when she does.

227. Find out who her favorite authors are and buy those books for her.

228. Find out her dreams and scheme to make them come true.

229. Make the bed in the morning.

230. Throw away your shitty, smelly, hole-filled old clothes.

231. Pick up your socks.

232. Get in shape and don't tell her about it.

233. Be successful in a way that her friends acknowledge her for.

234. Take her to the art museum or to the opera.

235. Find a way to make her laugh every day.

236. Climb a mountain (doesn't matter how big, just get above tree line) and vow to her that you love her more than as far as she can see.

237. Go on a whale watch with her.

238. Get a constellation map of the stars, and star gaze with her.

239. Take twenty pounds of Scotts turf builder and using your spreader spell out I LOVE YOU. Wait two weeks and watch what happens!

240. Do a chore that she would normally do—like the laundry, dishes, or dusting.

241. Take a picture that she treasures, and put it on a sheet of postage stamps (www.photostamps.com). Take one off the sheet, put the rest in a nice card, and mail it to her.

242. Tell her she is irreplaceable.

243. Tell her she brings light into your life.

244. Tell her you are lucky to have her.

245. Tell her you would be nothing without her.

246. Ask for her advice. Be sincere.

247. Share a special moment with her.

248. Go to www.puzzle-maker.com/cw/and build a romantic crossword puzzle for her. This site lets you take clues and answers and then reformats them into a crossword puzzle with the Down and Across clues below. Hint: use your pet names, the location of your honeymoon, favorite songs, etc. For a variation, use clues that are sensuous and suggestive and see what happens! We particularly like using rock 'n' roll songs (which all seem to be about sex and love and urgency!).

249. Ask her what would make her smile or feel special—go ahead, cheat. All's fair in this game.

250. Replace or fix something dear to her that is lost or broken.

Resources

Men's Weekends and Training

BetterMen Retreat—Wayne Levine

MDI Legacy Discovery Weekend—Men's Divisions International

Men's Rites of Passage—Center for Action and Contemplation run by Fr. Richard Rohr

New Warrior Training—The Mankind Project

Sterling Men's Weekend—Sterling Institute of Relationships—A. Justin Sterling

WEB SITES

http://www.malespirituality.org/ – Father Richard Rohr has perhaps the best blend of masculinity and spirituality that we know, and is the only place that also focuses on the training and initiation of elders among men.

http://www.bettermen.org/ – Wayne runs men's weekends and teaches/coaches men in the Southern California area.

http://www.sterling-institute.com/ – The Sterling Men's Weekend has been around since the early '80s and packs a lot of power into the initiation of men over a one weekend setting

http://mankindproject.org/ – The men who run the New Warrior Training—great men's support organization.

http://www.marriagemax.com/ Mort Fertel's Web site advertising his coaching for Marriage Fitness, but also has daily tips.

http://www.fathersandfamilies.org/ F&F – It is a resource for and lobbies actively for legislation to support fathers in divorce.

http://www.mensresourcesinternational.org/ – For the more higher purposed and globally focused among us, this is a great men's organization doing some very important work.

http://www.secretsofmarriedmen.com/ – Dr Scott Haltzman's Web site mostly hypes his book, but it's filled with tips and ideas.

http://www.mdisuccess.com/ – An excellent website to understand and find a men's team in your area.

http://www.ammsg.com/ – Our website listing tips, ideas and great links

Recommended Books for Your Shelf

Bly, Robert, *Iron John*, Vintage/Random House, New York, NY, 1990, 1992

Bly, Robert, *The Rag and Bone Shop of the Heart*, Harper Perennial, New York, NY, 1992

Deida, David, *Way of the Superior Man*, Sounds True, Boulder, CO, 1997, 2004

Levine, Wayne, *Hold on to Your N.U.T.s*; A Relationship Manual for Men, BetterMen Press, Agora Hills, CA, 2007

Moore, Robert and Douglas Gillette, *Warrior, King Lover, Magician*, Harper Collins, New York, NY, 1990

Real, Terrence, *I Don't Want to Talk About It*, Scribner, New York, NY, 1997

Rohr, Richard, *Adam's Return*, Spiritual Promises of Male Initiation, St. Anthony Messenger Press, Cincinnati, OH, 2006

Rohr, Richard, *Wild Man to Wise Man*, St. Anthony Messenger Press, Cincinnati, OH, 1990

Words to Live By

We sought out famous quotes for our chapter headings but found that we could not fit all of them in. So as an extra bonus, here are some of the others along with some of our own that we found to be simply good words to live by. Find a few that ring true for you and tape them to your computer screen or your bathroom mirror as a reminder of what you are up to:

- A man's track record means nothing to the feminine. A man could be perfect for ten years, but if he is an asshole for thirty seconds, his woman acts like he's always been one. David Deida
- Never assume that you fully know your woman—or any woman for that matter! A Married Man's Survival Guide
- A woman will forgive a man anything, except his failure to ask to be forgiven. Rumi
- The ultimate survival of your relationship depends on your discipline. A Married Man's Survival Guide
- Men always want to be a woman's first love—women like to be a man's last romance. Oscar Wilde

- Balanced masculinity is not embracing your "feminine" but rather learning to balance strength (your dick) with softness (your balls); power with vulnerability. A Married Man's Survival Guide

- To be happy with a man you must understand him a lot and love him a little. To be happy with a woman you must love her a lot and not try to understand her at all. Helen Rowland

- If a man prioritizes his relationship over his highest purpose, he weakens himself and cheats his woman. A Married Man's Survival Guide

- We come to love not by finding a perfect person, but by learning to see an imperfect person perfectly. Sam Keen

- Denying the fact that you have a killer inside of you, and failing to know him will inevitably result in his manifesting at the worst time. A Married Man's Survival Guide

- Man can never be a woman's equal in the spirit of selfless service with which nature has endowed her. Mohandas Gandhi

- Don't expect your wife to be your mother and don't demand that the relationship provide you with what your men should do. A Married Man's Survival Guide

- Your task is not to seek for love, but merely to seek and find all the barriers within yourself that you have built against it. Rumi

- Stop looking for logical explanations as to why she feels the way she does—emotions are not logical. A Married Man's Survival Guide

- Women are meant to be loved, not to be understood. Oscar Wilde

- Rule #1: No affairs except the one you have with your wife. Remember how to seduce her. A Married Man's Survival Guide

- Relationships are made of talk, and talk is for girls and women. Deborah Tannen

- Practice the five principles of the Art of War: Righteousness, Timing, Location, Leadership, and Execution. A Married Man's Survival Guide

- You'll never get what you really want. All you can do is give what you really want! David Deida

- When your wife tells you how she feels, she is just giving you a status report. A Married Man's Survival Guide

- A woman's sense of self is defined through her feelings and the quality of her relationships. John Gray

- The greatest skill you can practice in a relationship is silent, attentive listening. Shut up and pay attention. A Married Man's Survival Guide

- Eve left Adam, to meet the Devil in private. Alexander Pope

- No matter what you do or how big the gift was, it only nets you one point. A Married Man's Survival Guide

- Anger is a necessary part of the dance of love. Without anger we have no fire, no thunder and lightning to defend the sanctuary of the self. Sam Keen

- Your woman possesses more skills and talents than you could possibly imagine. Don't try to compete or measure up—it is a waste of time for you and demeaning to her. A Married Man's Survival Guide

- When women go wrong, men go right after them. Mae West

- Each woman is three women: a queen, a little girl, and a wild woman yearning to break the rules. A Married Man's Survival Guide
- Women are never disarmed by compliments. Men always are. Oscar Wilde
- A woman's primary sexual organ is her mind. A Married Man's Survival Guide
- You can ravish your woman so deeply that her surrender breaks your heart into light. David Deida
- Make sex about her—the more you focus on her need, the more she can and will surrender. A Married Man's Survival Guide
- Women give to men the very gold of their lives. But they invariably want it back in such very small change. Oscar Wilde
- Her upsetness need not be yours—practice keeping that perspective so that you can respond appropriately A Married Man's Survival Guide
- Plane crashes are more likely to be the result of an accumulation of minor difficulties and seemingly trivial malfunctions any one of which, by itself, would not be problematic. Malcolm Gladwell
- What you say doesn't matter—it's what you do and continue to do consistently that will make the difference A Married Man's Survival Guide
- Strength does not come from physical capacity. It comes from an indomitable will. Mohandas Gandhi
- Regaining your woman's trust requires consistent behavior over an extended period of time A Married Man's Survival Guide

- A woman under stress is not immediately concerned with finding solutions to her problems but rather seeks relief by expressing herself and being understood. John Gray
- It is not a matter of "if" she will find out about your affair, it is only a matter of "when"—don't go there. A Married Man's Survival Guide
- You know who must be very secure in their masculinity? Male ladybugs. Jay Leno
- When you stop focusing on your woman, you lose the capacity to be enchanted and infatuated by her—do one thing each day exclusively for her and watch what happens to you. A Married Man's Survival Guide

References and Works Cited

Armstrong, Alison A., *Making Sense of Men, A Woman's Guide to a Lifetime of Love, Care and Attention from All Men*, PAX Programs, Inc., Sherman Oaks, CA, 2007

Bly, Robert, James Hillman and Michael Meade *The Rag and Bone Shop of the Heart, Poems for Men*, Harper Perennial, New York, NY, 1992

Brizendine, Louann, *The Female Brain*, Broadway Books, New York, NY, 2006

Children's Justice online source at http://www.childrensjustice.org/stats.htm

Chapman, Gary, *The Five Love Languages, Men's Edition*, Northfield Publishing, Chicago, IL, 2004

Chin-Ning Chu, *The Art of War for Women*, Random House/Currency Books, New York, NY, 2007

DeAngelis, Barbara, *What Women Want Men to Know: the Ultimate Book about Love, Sex, and Relationships for You*, Hyperion, New York, NY, 2001

Gray, John, *Men Are From Mars, Women Are From Venus*, HarperCollins, New York, NY, 1992

Godek, Gregory J.P., *Romantic Fantasies, & Other Sexy Ways of Expressing Your Love*, Casablanca Press, Naperville, IL, 1997

Gottman, J.M., *What Predicts Divorce?* Lawrence Earlbaum, Hillsdale, NJ, 1994

Hallowell, Edward M., M.D. and Susan Hallowell, *Married to Distraction: Restoring Intimacy and Strengthening Your Marriage in an Age of Interruption*, Random House, New York, NY, 2010

Levine, Wayne M., *Hold On To Your N.U.T.s, The Relationship Manual For Men*, BetterMen Press, Austin, TX, 2007

Moore, Robert and Douglas Gillette, "Initiation and the Male Spiritual Quest," in *Redeeming Men: Religion and Masculinities*, Stephen Boyd, et al., eds., Westminster John Knox Press, Louisville, KY, 1996, pp.187-196

Moore, Robert and Douglas Gillette, *Warrior, King Lover, Magician*, Harper Collins, New York, NY, 1990

Nair, Keshavan, *A Higher Standard of Leadership, Lessons from the life of Gandhi*, Berrett-Koehler Publishers, San Francisco, CA, 1994

Poem Hunter: http://www.poemhunter.com/poem/all-which-isn-t-singing-is-mere-talking/

Pruett, Kyle and Kline Pruett, Marsha, *Partnership Parenting, How Men and Women Parent Differently—Why It Helps Kids and Can Strengthen Your Marriage*, Da Capo Press, Cambridge, MA, 2009

Rohr, Richard, *Adam's Return, The Five Promises of Male Initiation*, New York, NY, Crossroad Publishing, 2004

Rohr, Richard, *Wild Man to Wise Man, Reflections in Male Spirituality*, Cincinnati OH, St. Anthony Messenger Press, 2005

Schwartz, Barry, *The Paradox of Choice, Why More is Less*, Harper Perennial, New York, NY, 2004

Sutton, Robert I, *The No Asshole Rule, Building a Civilized Workplace and Surviving One That Isn't*, Warner Business Books, New York, NY, 2007

Tannen, Deborah, *That's Not What I Meant*, Ballantine Books, New York, NY, 1986

Tannen, Deborah, *You Just Don't Understand, Women and Men in Conversation*, Ballantine Books, New York, NY, 1991

BIOS

<u>Kris Girrell</u>—Now in his third marriage, Kris has over three decades of married life experience—nearly two-thirds of which successfully in his current and last ever. Figuring the first two marriages taught the hard lessons, Kris' present marriage "works because we work it!" He first got involved in men's work in 1979, and has led workshops and been a member of a men's team/circle ever since. In his day job, Kris is an Executive Leadership Coach with a consulting firm in Boston, Massachusetts. He is the author of a book and many articles in his profession, contributes regularly to local papers with op-ed commentary, and actively blogs on several topics. At the age of sixty, he has re-entered college for yet another degree, this time in the field of Theology, and has just been awarded a First Degree Black Belt in TaeKwonDo.

Kris lives with his wife and twelve-year-old son in Andover, Massachusetts, and has two married adult daughters and two grandchildren.

<u>David Plante</u> first engaged in Men's Work when he took part in the Sterling Men's Weekend in 1999. He has held many positions of

leadership within local and regional men's groups. Dave has taught men's growth and development classes, has led teams and groups in charitable projects and been a major force in western Massachusetts. In addition, Dave is currently a member of the Civil Air Patrol, responsible for recruitment.

Dave is married and has been with the same woman for twenty years this past October. As the father of three children, Dave's passion here has always been trying to understand what a successful family and marriage looks like.

In business, Dave has successfully run his own company for eight years, employs five people, and has a history of exceeding customers' expectations. His company sells, services, and repairs Point of Sale computers and touch screens for restaurants and is currently responsible for keeping over 2100 computers up and running twenty-four hours a day. Dave is an avid coin collector and enjoys tinkering with things, especially those things he has no intention of putting back together.

Made in the USA
Charleston, SC
30 May 2011